Along the Neva

Along the Neva

GERMAN PARATROOPS
OF THE 1ST BATTALION 3RD FALLSCHIRMJÄGER REGIMENT ON THE RUSSIAN FRONT SEPTEMBER-NOVEMBER 1941

Edgar Alcidi

Schiffer Military History
Atglen, PA

Ackowledgments

Special thanks to Herr Friedrich Else and Gottfried Emrich who shared with me their war diaries. A special thank also to Wilhelm Knoche. Their memories made this book possible.

Friedrich "Fritz" Else. (F.Else)

Gottfried Emrich. (G.Emrich)

Thanks to: Eric Queen, your amazing book *Red Shines The Sun* remains my inspiration. Thanks also to: Chris Mason, Rob Hanneman, Stephan Janzyk, Ulrich Dübi. Frau Kuhl Bundesarchiv Koblenz, Herr Koch Bundesarchiv Freiburg. Falko Heitmann, Steffen Rhode and Bund Deutscher Fallschirmjäger e.V. Thanks also to Shaun Winkler for his help and friendship. Darlene Waldschmidt-Sematat, thanks for all the translating work.

Dedication

In memory of Herr Heinz Glüsen.

Book design by Robert Biondi.

Library of Congress Catalog Number: 2010934290.

Printed in China.
ISBN: 978-0-7643-3657-7

Published by Schiffer Publishing Ltd.
4880 Lower Valley Road
Atglen, PA 19310
Phone: (610) 593-1777
FAX: (610) 593-2002
E-mail: Info@schifferbooks.com.
Visit our web site at: www.schifferbooks.com
Please write for a free catalog.
This book may be purchased from the publisher.
Please include $5.00 postage.
Try your bookstore first.

In Europe, Schiffer books are distributed by:
Bushwood Books
6 Marksbury Ave.
Kew Gardens, Surrey TW9 4JF
England
Phone: 44 (0)20 8392-8585
FAX: 44 (0)20 8392-9876
E-mail: info@bushwoodbooks.co.uk
www.bushwoodbooks.co.uk

Contents

1

The Situation: September 1941

On June 22, 1941, the Germans invaded Russia; that was the beginning of "Operation Barbarossa". The German troops were divided into three groups: Army Groups North, Centre and South.

The goal of Army Group North – which consisted of the 16th Army and the 18th Army as well as the 4th Panzer group – was Leningrad. Altogether it encompassed twenty-nine divisions with over 500,000 men. Its commander was *Feldmarschall* Ritter von Leeb.

Leeb's orders were to destroy the Russian troops in the Baltic region and to occupy Riga, the capital city of Latvia. The city was captured on June 29th and therefore the first goal of the Germans was accomplished. In early July the German Wehrmacht continued their advance, and on the evening of July 8th the 4th Panzer Group (*Generaloberst* Erich Hoepner) arrived at Lake Peipus and thus successfully achieved its second intended goal. But in the meantime, the first problems with ensuring adequate supplies were encountered.

The infantry divisions toiled northwards through the Riga region on foot and were not able to keep up with the panzer units, even though they had walked 350km in eleven days. At that point it already become clear that the invasion plans had considerably under-estimated the vastness of the Russian territory.

The width of the frontline of Army Group North had increased from the initial 120km to a width of approximately 600km. But while the resistance of the Russians was getting more tenacious, the German troops had not received reinforcements in the meantime. There was dogged fighting for every village. The terrain with its forested and swampy areas impeded the attacks of the Germans who were frequently embroiled in bitter close combat. Nevertheless, on August 17th units of the 291st Infantry Division (*Generalleutnant* Kurt Herzog) under *Oberst* Lohmeyer captured Narva. However a considerable amount of time had been lost because of the heavy fighting. And by this time the German troops were completely exhausted.

On the other side, those battles were more than welcomed by the Russian leaders. They were able to take advantage of that valuable time to fortify their line of defence around Leningrad. More than 200,000 workers were deployed each day to do the work. Within a short time they had built a line of defence consisting of anti-tank ditches 600km long, as well as more than 4,000 bunkers and 600 machine gun emplacements. In spite of all the difficulties, the Germans still kept up their forward movement. *Feldmarschall* von Leeb was in the process of planning an offensive thrust towards Leningrad, when bad news suddenly arrived. The flank of the 16th Army south of Lake Ilmen was endangered by the rapid attack of the 38th Russian Army. The situation was so serious that the entire front was at risk. Therefore, Army Group North was forced to react as fast as possible to avoid being cut off from Army Group Centre. Several units immediately redeployed from the Leningrad area, heading toward Lake Ilmen. This meant that the 4th Panzer Group alone had lost fifty percent of its troops! The compact, concentrated attack that von Leeb wanted no longer seemed possible. So establishing a fast connection with the Finnish along Lake Ladoga became even more necessary for the Germans. Thus, the battle for the Luga position had begun. The rain in the last days of August had thoroughly soaked the roads. Mud delayed the delivery of supplies, because vehicles as well as the guns were constantly getting bogged down. The fierce fighting lasted until Luga fell on August 25th. The Germans took more than 20,000 Russian prisoners in the Luga pocket alone.

Army Group North then headed out, marching towards Lake Ladoga. After fierce fighting in the area of Sinyavino, the Germans finally managed to break through on September 8th. They ultimately reached the south side of Lake Ladoga and captured the town of Schlisselburg. The consequence was that shipping traffic from Lake Ladoga was blocked.

The frontal attack on Leningrad began only twenty-four hours later. Huge difficulties were to be expected, and those expectations proved to be true – with a vengeance. Every single metre mattered to the Russians. The Russian artillery inflicted heavy losses on the attacking Germans, whereby some infantry companies only had thirty men left.

By making strenuous efforts, on September 17th the Germans succeeded in seizing the summer residence of the Russian Tsar, but in the course of the same day the already tense situation changed abruptly for the Germans. Order No.35 had to be executed with immediate effect. But what did that mean? On September 6th in Order No.35, Hitler ordered the commanders of the German Armed Forces to capture Moscow before the winter. For Army Group North that meant that capturing Leningrad became a matter of secondary importance. On that same day, tank units as well as other units had to withdraw from the Leningrad area and prepare themselves for evacuation. Under those circumstances, launching additional attacks on Leningrad was no longer possible. So the siege of the city began. In spite of Russian efforts, Leningrad was still completely surrounded and could only be supplied from the air and by way of Lake Ladoga. In the meantime, the Russian command had recognised the German weakness and on September 22nd launched an attack south of Schlisselburg. That was the location of the so-called "bottleneck" – a 14 to 15km wide corridor leading to Lake Ladoga.

Almost at the same time, the 52nd Russian Army stormed in from the east. The objective of the attack was to break through the ring surrounding the city and to annihilate the 18th German Army using a pincer strategy. During that attack the losses of the Germans were so massive that the command had doubts about whether it would even be possible to hold the front any longer. Under those circumstances the high command of the Wehrmacht needed to take action as fast as possible in order to cope with these developments. Reinforcements had to be moved to the front as soon as possible. In the view of the German command, the paratroopers seemed to be especially suitable. On the evening of September 24th, the 1st Paratrooper Regiment received orders for air transport. The 2nd Battalion of the *Sturmregiment* was made available to Regiment 1 for this deployment instead of the otherwise deployed 2nd Battalion. The mission of the 2nd Battalion of the *Sturmregiment* was to eliminate a bridgehead that the Russians had established at Petrushino.

The Battalion, reinforced by the 2nd Company Anti-Tank Unit 7, attacked the bridgehead without any special reconnaissance or preparation. The attack was impeded by thick fog and came to a standstill in spite of its momentum and speed. There was also a lack of heavy weapons and artillery. The paratroopers mounted attacks again and again but they were invariably repelled. It was a desperate struggle for mere survival – usually hand-to-hand fighting – with paratroopers bleeding to death without succeeding in eliminating the bridgehead.

The battalion lost all of its officers through death or injury. Its commander – *Major* Edgar Stenzler, a holder of the Knight's Cross – died from wounds.

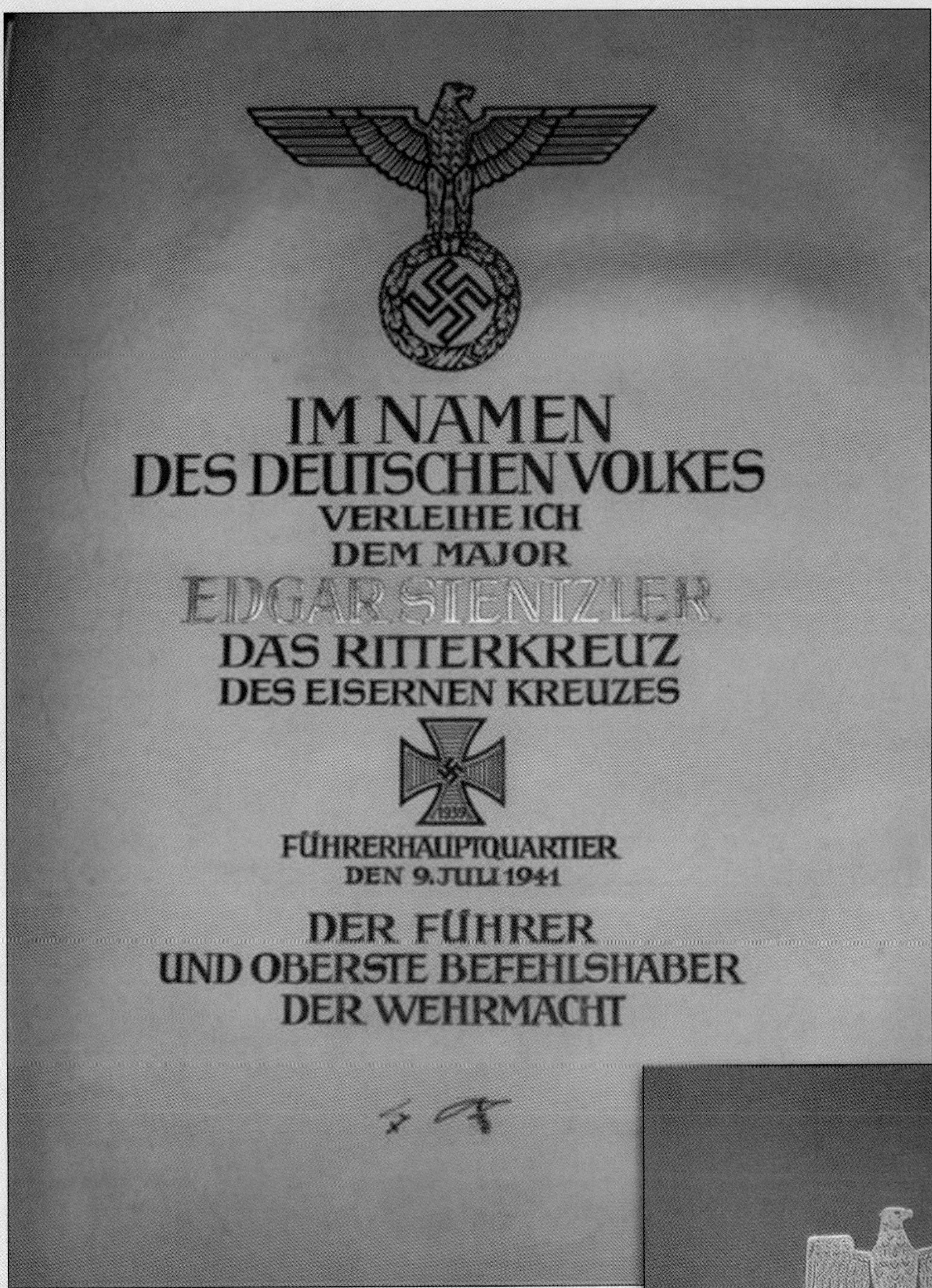

IM NAMEN
DES DEUTSCHEN VOLKES
VERLEIHE ICH
DEM MAJOR
EDGAR STENZLER
DAS RITTERKREUZ
DES EISERNEN KREUZES

FÜHRERHAUPTQUARTIER
DEN 9. JULI 1941

DER FÜHRER
UND OBERSTE BEFEHLSHABER
DER WEHRMACHT

Major Edgar Stenzler's Knight's Cross parchment in red leather folder. (Rob Hanneman)

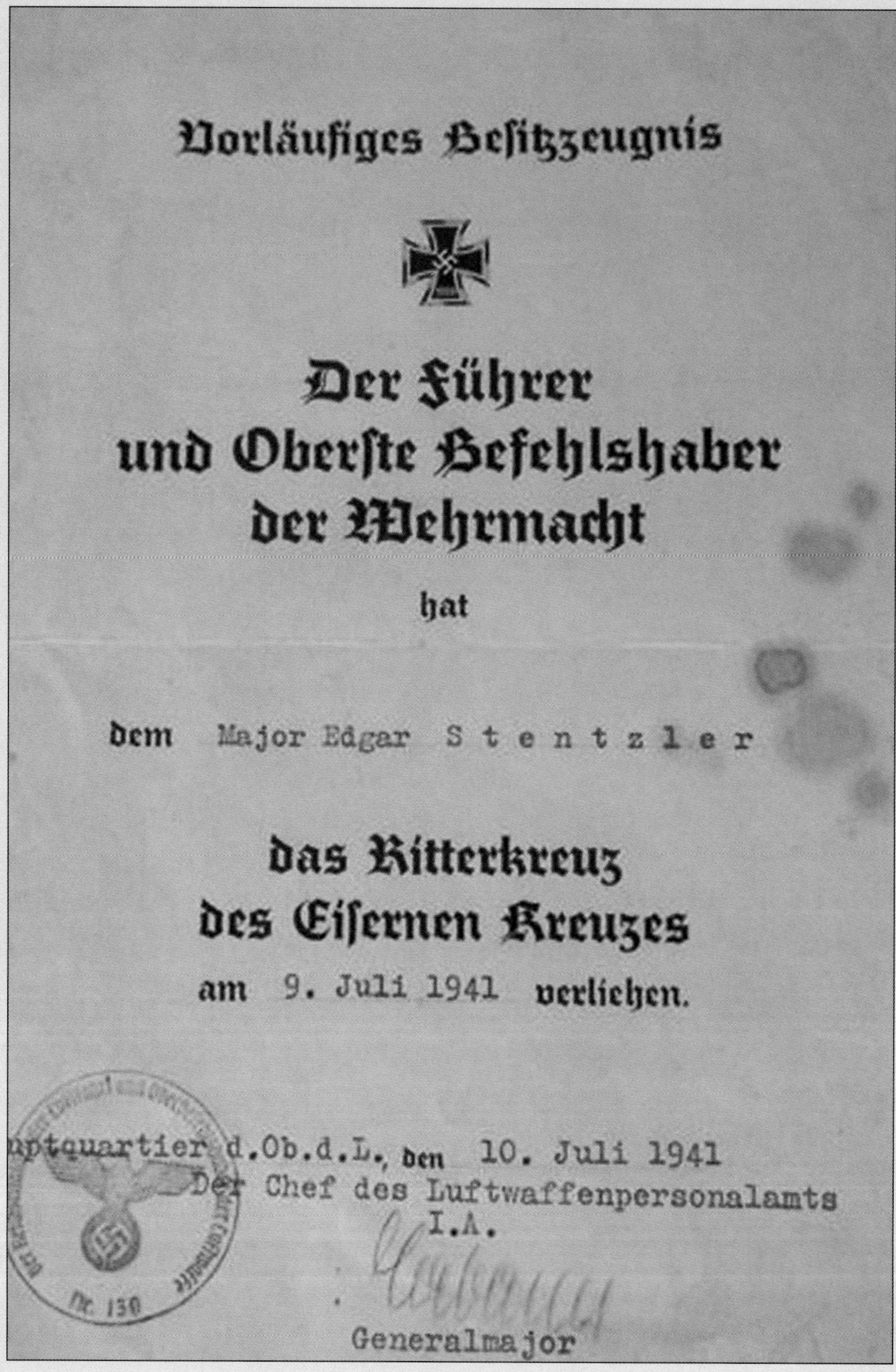

Vorläufiges Besitzzeugnis

Der Führer
und Oberste Befehlshaber
der Wehrmacht

hat

dem Major Edgar S t e n t z l e r

das Ritterkreuz
des Eisernen Kreuzes
am 9. Juli 1941 verliehen.

ptquartier d.Ob.d.L., den 10. Juli 1941
Der Chef des Luftwaffenpersonalamts
I.A.

Generalmajor

Nr. 130

Stenzler's Knight's Cross award. (Rob Hanneman)

Portrait of Edgar Stenzler wearing the Knight's Cross earned for actions on Crete. (Rob Hanneman)

Eduard Leopold Edgar Stenzler was born in Dortmund March 27, 1905. (Rob Hanneman)

Thus, it became clear that the 1st Paratrooper Regiment would not be able to cope with the serious crisis on its own. But instead of deploying the entire Flieger-Division 7, the 3rd Regiment was moved to the front with additional units following.

The 1st Battalion (I./Rgt.3) was alerted at the training base at Grafenwöhr (Upper Palatinate) and had to be relocated to Russia as fast as possible. At the end of September, the paratroopers from Grafenwöhr travelled by train as far as Neuhausen near Königsberg (East Prussia). Several units were air lifted to Russia from their home base in Wolfenbüttel. Then on October 3rd they flew from an airfield close to Neuhausen to Pleskau (today's Pskov) and from there they continued on to Luban (Lyuban) on October 4th.

2

Organisation of the 1st Battalion Regiment 3 (I./Rgt.3)

Battalion Commander: *Hauptmann* Friedrich August von der Heydte
Adjutant: *Oberleutnant* Kurt Lauk
Staff officer: *Oberleutnant* Kurt Veth

Kompanie (1st Company): *Oberleutnant* Hepke
Kompanie (2nd Company): *Oberleutnant* Wilhelm Knoche
Kompanie (3rd Company): *Oberleutnant* Straehler-Pohl
Kompanie (4th Company): *Oberleutnant* Adolf Peiser

Organisation of the 4th company:

2IC: *Hauptfeldwebel* Link

Platoon leader:
1.) Körner
2.) Ackermann
3.) Golz
4.) Möck

Members of 1st. Company. Note the Kleeblatt (clover leaf) tactical symbol on the wall. (Author)

The officers of I./Rgt.3, from left to right: ?, Lt. Krüger, ?, Olt. Straehler-Pohl, Hptm. Freiherr von der Heydte, Lt. Lauk, Lt. Peiser. (Author)

Hans Hammermann paymaster (Zahlmeister) of I./Rgt.3. (Author)

On the way to Russia; in front Gefr. Renner, right Gefr. Else. (Emrich)

4th Kp. with the train to Russia. (Emrich)

Gottfried Emrich wearing Kreta cufftitle and Ground Assault Badge. (Emrich)

Oberleutnant Wilhelm Knoche, Commander of 2./Rgt.3. (BA Freiburg)

Friedrich Else as a Gefreiter. (Else)

3rd October, the 4th company in Pleskau. (Emrich)

Signposts in Mga. Note the directional sign to Schlisselburg. (Author)

Paratroopers on the way to the front. Note the four-leaf clover sign (Rgt.3) at left. (Private Collection)

A Russian village. (Author)

Paratroopers inspecting a village. (BA Koblenz 0101-548-0702-27)

Advanced positions close to the Neva river – the enemy is just on the other side. (Author)

Fallschirmjäger marching to the front. (Author)

Kurt Veth here with MP looking for new positions. (Author)

The battlefield. (BA Freiburg)

Inside a paratrooper trench. (BA Freiburg)

Bunker of I.Rgt.3. (Author)

Oberleutnant Veth near a sign with the word, 'Jungfernsteig' ('Remember the street in Hamburg'). (Author)

A Fallschirmjäger with his best friend. (Author)

3

Petrushino

The survivors of II.*Sturmregiment* withstood the pressure of the Soviet forces and prevented the Russians from breaking out of the bridgehead until the I./Rgt.3 under *Hauptmann* von der Heydte finally appeared on the scene and took over the endangered sector.

Gottfried Emrich, an *Oberjäger* in the 4th Company, reminisces:

"We arrived in Pleskau on October 3rd. During the flight, we were able to see quite a lot of the whole miserable situation, because the plane flew through a partisans' area, hugging the terrain. Quite frequently we could clearly see systems of fortified positions and supply convoys far below us.

"Towards the evening we were driven to unoccupied barracks on the edge of town. The barracks looked like a prison – very thick walls, no windows. Some of us preferred to lie down outside – so did I – we were afraid of fleas. In the morning we were driven back to the airfield. Our flight took us over forests and fields and finally got us to Luban. The airfield at Luban was quite busy and crowded. Everything was happening in great haste. We quickly unloaded our planes and boarded the heavy transport vehicles that had been provided by the infantry. Our plane was immediately reloaded with wounded men. The impression we got was that the whole situation was pretty dicey. We could already hear the thunder of cannons from far away.

"For several hours we drove along bad roads – over log causeways and through forests. Our convoy was frequently forced to take cover and hide from Russian planes. The driver of the transporter said: 'Leningrad is over there.' Then we reached our destination – just before it got dark. The drivers said that they could not drive the vehicles any further.

Everything ahead of us was quiet. There was only a constant thumping sound coming from the right. We crawled into the roadside ditch on the left to lie down and started rooting through our provisions. We had been supplied with really great stuff again – ham, dextrose, cheese, an iron ration (one kg tin of pork), chocolate. We loaded our weapons and made sure they were ready to fire. That was the first time that we were carrying sharpened bayonets with us. Our entrenchment tools ("Schanzzeug") were also sharpened (Note: The sharpened folding spade proved to be an excellent weapon for close combat. It often had to be used as a pick in the frozen sandy soil of Russia. When using it like that we found that it was necessary to reinforce the handle.).

"This time we were deployed as a signal squadron. I was allocated to the company's command post together with my unit. Just like with every other deployment, our pay book was replaced by airmen's identification documents. Then we waited for it to get completely dark before taking up our positions. The other signal corps units were allocated to the mortar platoon and the machine gun (SMG). It was October 5th. After marching through the forest in the dead of night for hours – stumbling and even falling – our company commander, Oberleutnant Adolf Peiser, allocated us to our position in a small wood together with a sub-machine gun platoon, the company unit and the signal corps. We did not notice any soldiers that were supposed to be relieved. In front of us there was a huge level plain covered in high grass. That was where the enemy was, somewhere over there. We built ourselves quite a large bunker between four large fir trees. We covered it up with branches and earth, and filled in the sides with brush-wood. Our battalion positioned itself in a semi-circle around a Russian bridgehead that had been established over the River Neva.

"When it got light we set up the communication line – which we had not found at night – to the mortar platoon, which had taken up a position in a sand pit. In order to get to that position, you had to cross an exposed area first. There was not much of a distance from there to the Russians. We had to be extremely cautious during our daily walk from our command post to the mortar platoon. Individual messengers often disappeared or men fetching food were shot and wounded. You kept stumbling over dead bodies. Dressing materials were lying around all over the place. We could no longer wash ourselves, and our beards were growing. Those were the days when the first snow fell, and the ground got wet and cold. We fortified our position very well; all of the bunkers were connected by trenches."

Friedrich Else, *Obergefreiter* from 4th Company, was also there:

"The convoy of heavy transport vehicles took us to a spot right behind the front. Our section under Feldwebel Rentsch was categorised as a "zbV" group. (Note: zur besondere Verfügung = for special purposes). That meant that we were put at the disposal of every company.

Building a position in Petruschino. At right is Oblt. Peiser. (Emrich)

Emrich's bunker with his crew in Petruschino. From left to right: Wagner, Fischer, Steinmann. (Emrich)

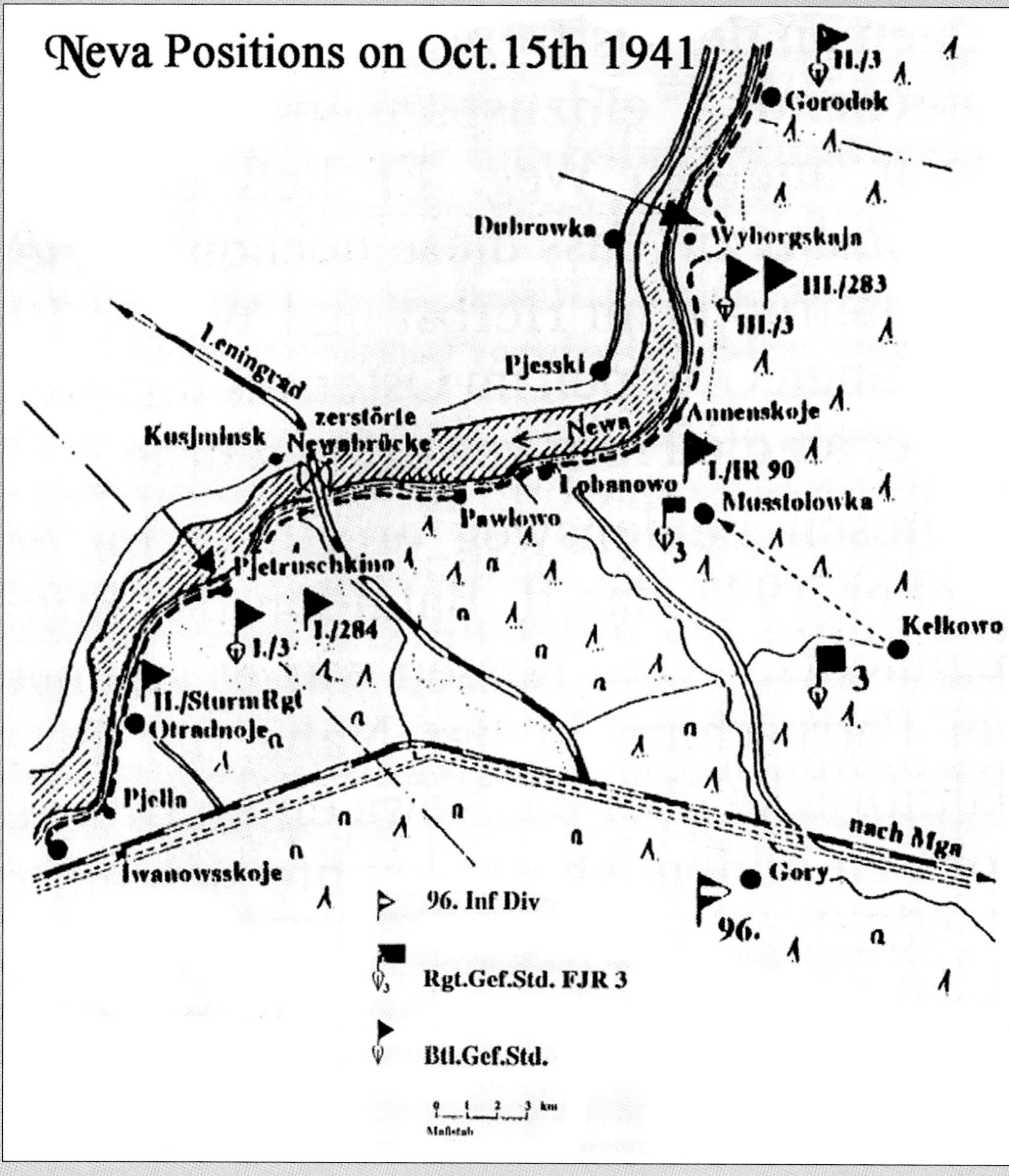
Neva Positions on Oct. 15th 1941
II./3
Gorodok
Dubrowka
Wyborgskaja
III./283
III./3
Leningrad
Pjesski
zerstörte
Newabrücke
Kusjmlnsk
Newa
Annenskoje
I./IR 90
Lobanowo
Musstolowka
Pawlowo
Pjetruschkino
I./284
I./3
Kelkowo
3
II./SturmRgt
Otradnoje
Pjella
Iwanowsskoje
nach Mga
Gory
96.
96. Inf Div
Rgt.Gef.Std. FJR 3
Btl.Gef.Std.
0 1 2 3 km
Maßstab

Positions in the sand pit. (Author)

New orders for the mortar crews at the sand pit. In the middle is Oberjäger Baumann (Emrich)

Trenches near the pit. (Author)

The enemy is very close. (Author)

Mortar crews in the sand pit of Petruschino. (Emrich)

Members of the 4th Kp. (Emrich)

An air-defense position. At left is Oblt. Peiser, on the right Gefr. Renner. (Emrich)

Gewehrgruppe Lammoth in Petruschino. From left to right: Van Koll, Elsner, Lammoth, Miesok, Hagemann, Else, Kern. (Else)

Awaiting the Russians. (Private Collection)

Relaxing with a pipe. (Private Collection)

"When Feldwebel Rentsch came back from the briefing by the company commander we were allocated to, it was already dark. He still briefed our two Gewehrführer (gun leader) Oberjäger Lammoth and Alois Gabmeier. Then we set off to the position allocated to us. Everything went off without a hitch. In a shallow ditch the 1st gunner (Schütze 1), Hagemann, and I set up our SMG (heavy machine gun) to be used in a kneeling position. Our Gewehrführer was lying to the right beside Hagemann and Hein van Koll was on my left, quite close to me. Hein was responsible for ammunition replenishment. The other three gunners – Franz Kern, Hein Misock and Elsner – were also lying close to us. Up to then, in spite of several artillery hits and a few hissing machine gun volleys from the Russians, everything was just like a weapons drill. But our tension was rising more and more. In the process, the 2nd Battalion of the Sturmregiment", which was fighting ahead of us, was ultimately annihilated. Dead Russians were still lying right beside our position. The Russians had probably not noticed our arrival as replacements because everything was quiet at the Russian position, which was 100m in front of us at the most."

Oberleutnant Wilhelm Knoche, the commander of the 2nd Company, recalls his arrival at Petrushino:

"Hauptmann von der Heydte inspected the front of the Stenzler Battalion together with his company commanders and assigned the companies their positions. The enemy artillery and mortar fire was pounding the German positions non-stop. That gave the officers a foretaste of what to expect there."

The 2nd Company under *Oberleutnant* Knoche, who – as senior company commander – was also the deputy of the battalion commander, was assigned to the central sector of the encircling ring. From then on it was destined to bear the main burden of the battle.

Oberleutnant Knoche continues:

"First of all, the objective was to fend off the constant thrusts of the enemy. Those thrusts were fought off with concentrated fire and heavy weapons that were in position on the other side of the bank of the Neva. What was characteristic about those attacks was that the target, namely the railway hub at Mga, a town that was about 12km away, was systematically hammered home to every single Red Army soldier at the bridgehead. Mga was a kind of 'fata morgana' for all of the Russians. The commissars told their men that they would find bread, potatoes, tobacco and above all vodka in incredible quantities there. In accordance with that misrepresentation, the men – who only had insufficient supplies – fought like berserks in order to capture that fabled land of plenty for themselves.

"It was necessary to pursue a clear strategy before the 1st Battalion could demolish the bridgehead. The sacrifice of the II. Sturmregiment demonstrated that the bridgehead could only be eliminated by means of a well-planned battle. The positions on the front were extremely muddled and distinguishing between friend and foe was next to possible. So the new objective was to establish a solid defensive front in order to take back the initiative and to be able to command flexibly again."

Oberleutnant Knoche continues:

"I set up my command post in a section of ditch covered with telephone poles. The disadvantage was that the enemy was dangerously close. But on the other hand the advantage was that I was in direct proximity to a battery that I could request as assistance by way of a communication line. The number of fallen soldiers was highly visible. The Russians and Germans were just lying next to and on top of each other, right where they had been cut down by bullets and grenades. Recovering or burying the fallen was not possible."

The battalion command repeatedly discovered that the troops had not acted correctly when recovering and burying the fallen. The papers of the dead were often removed and identification tags were torn off, or completely removed before the bodies were buried. That made identification much more difficult later on.

Oberleutnant Knoche had the sad duty of recovering and burying the body of *Leutnant* Alex Dick, whom he knew personally. *Leutnant* Dick was born in St. Petersburg and died close to his birthplace. At that time *Hauptmann* von der Heydte attempted to get effective artillery support. This was his absolute top priority in order to prevent the battalion from suffering the same fate as Battalion Stenzler. He eventually succeeded, and then the I. Btl. was able to count on artillery support if needed.

After thorough reconnaissance the order to attack was issued.

Oberleutnant Knoche describes how he experienced the attack:

"After a burst of fire from all the heavy weapons that were available at the bridgehead, after nightfall my 2nd Company was supposed to launch a frontal attack, and the 1st and 3rd Companies were supposed to attack from the flank on the right and left respectively and squeeze the bridgehead in a pincer movement, while the fire from heavy weapons was supposed to rain down on the other side of the Neva in order to prevent the enemy from moving reserves and supplies forward."

SMG position of Hein van Koll (left), and Friedrich Else. (Emrich)

Heinz Glüsen (with pipe) in a foxhole with Kruggel. (BDF)

Camouflaged position. (Author)

Gefreiter Heinz Glüsen in Petruschino (4./Rgt.3). (BDF)

Oberjäger Heini Kruggel (4th company). (BDF)

Trench in Petruschino. (Emrich)

Inside the Stab Bunker. (Author)

Oblt. Veth map reading inside a bunker. (Author)

Handmade sign outside the bunker. (Author)

Recon in enemy territory. (BA Koblenz 183-B18801)

The village of Petrushino, which was right in the middle of the bridgehead, had been burned and totally razed to the ground. It also offered absolutely no advantages – neither for the attackers nor defenders. At dawn *Hauptmann* von der Heydte inspected the starting positions in order to make sure that everybody had understood the attack order properly.

He discussed every single phase of the enterprise once again with *Oberleutnant* Knoche and his platoon leaders. When the hour struck at the agreed upon time, a dense burst of fire rained down on the surprised enemy at the bridgehead.

The paratroopers' attack immediately gained ground and reached the Russian positions in a storm-like advance. A number of surprised Red Army soldiers surrendered without any resistance whatsoever, but a complete collapse of the line was not destined to happen. Instead the resistance of the Russians grew stronger and an increase in their defensive efforts from the steep slope of the bank of the Neva was observable.

However, the enemy was not able to withstand the paratroopers' attack and the latter succeeded in prevailing in hand-to-hand fighting. Within the semicircular bridgehead, the 1st, with the 3rd Company on the wings of the attack line, only had a relatively short distance to cover before getting to the bank of the Neva, and they reached the river together with the right and left wings of the 2nd Company and took a large number of prisoners. However, in the middle the attack thrust encountered fierce resistance and began to falter. Even the reserve troops that were deployed were not able to achieve any success. *Oberleutnant* Knoche gave the order to "Dig in and hold!" the positions that had been taken.

Obergefreiter Else was in the dugout:

"Our instructions were: Clear some space for our attacking riflemen by firing during the impending night-time attack so that the Russians would have to take cover for five minutes (that was called scatter fire), with side stops and a setting aimed low. The light from the large numbers of signal rockets made it easy to make out the ground. The attack was scheduled to start at 10:00p.m. Our riflemen had worked their way forward until they were quite close to the Russians. We and the artillery opened up with a curtain fire right on time after the first red flare (Note: at the beginning, the paratroopers and the Russians were using the same colours for their signal flares. That frequently led to misunderstandings, so that the barrage that was observed was triggered mistakenly and/or there was no order to start it). After five minutes we stopped immediately after a green-and-red signal rocket. The riflemen pushed their way into the Russian positions, loudly yelling 'Hurrah!' Hagemann and I were given the order: 'Stop and full cover'. Then Hagemann made a big mistake: He folded up the right rear strut of the gun carriage. The machine gun tipped over – the casing and

barrel red hot – and fell into the sand. To the right of us the attack was in full swing. At that moment our battalion commander von der Heydte suddenly appeared right next to us. He immediately issued the order:

"'Everybody come with me – except the MG team!' During the fire attack together with Hein van Koll I had attached three belt straps with 300 shots each, which is what had made the barrel get red hot. Now our machine gun was only able to shoot single shots. I tried to get our machine gun fixed, which was actually the responsibility of the 1st gunner.

"Suddenly, I heard something pretty unbelievable. In spite of the battle noise I heard Männe (Hagemann) snoring. At the same moment I suddenly saw a couple Russians, right in our sights, coming towards us and loudly yelling 'Hurrah!'

"I cried out: 'Männe, Männe, either duck or keep shooting until our pistols are empty!' We shot until we had emptied our pistols and magazines. The Russians turned aside or fell.

"Towards 2.00 a.m. things started to quiet down a bit."

Early in the morning the Russians launched fierce counter attacks, but they broke down under the paratrooper's defensive fire. Then when the paratroopers launched a counter-thrust, they were caught lying in the fire from the Russian artillery. Two days went by without anything changing substantially. *Oberleutnant* Hepke became ill, *Oberleutnant* Knoche took over the 1st Company and then his deputy, *Leutnant* Werner Krüger, led the 2nd Company. The preparations for finally eliminating the bridgehead were not yet completed when a number of Russians defected to the 2nd Company at dusk. *Leutnant* Krüger instructed *Feldwebel* Scholz to question the defectors. Scholz spoke Russian fluently and found out that when they were escaping the defectors had shot a "commissar" who was the backbone of the resistance. *Leutnant* Krüger immediately sent *Feldwebel* Scholz forward with two of the defectors and had the Russians deliver the request for surrender. And the impossible actually happened. The Russians crawled out of their holes, lifted their hands up and climbed down the steep slope of the Neva, heading for imprisonment.

Russian artillery on the other riverbank then started shooting at the masses of surrendering Russians. But they were no longer able to prevent the capitulation. During those hits the battalion's physician – Dr. Petrisch – fell as well. A shell fragment penetrated his heart while he was treating a casualty.

The day after that the enemy had been cleared out of the Petrushino bridgehead completely. *Hauptmann* von der Heydte was awarded the German Cross in Gold for his achievement and for that of his men.

Oberjäger Emrich describes those days:

"So the bridgehead no longer existed at that part of the front. Our company had established a position on the riverbank. The sub machine guns were also brought into position. We set up a communication line from that position at the extreme forefront back to our command post. We attributed the extraordinarily good marksmanship of the Russian artillery during the previous days to the following: a Russian captain who was presumed to be dead had been lying there for several days. Then someone nudged him by accident and it turned out that he was still alive. He had had a radio set hidden underneath his body. Where we were things got quiet again. But up front every night the Russians tried to cross the river with boats and rafts that were camouflaged to look like bits of floating islands. But annihilating fire succeeded in turning them back again and again. Then in the evening we always heard German march music from Russian loudspeakers that had been set up, along with propaganda about our hopeless situation and the promising opportunities offered by defecting. Our answer to that propaganda was a creeping barrage. Our communication line was constantly being interrupted by harassing fire from the Russians. So we flitted back and forth. When it suddenly got dark, we tried to follow the line back to our command post, holding on to it with one hand. When we got close to our sentries that were posted, we (Jäger Müller and I) purposely spoke very clearly to make sure we were recognised. Somebody suddenly fired a shot without calling out 'Halt!' But thank God he missed. The sentry had been sleeping and, when we startled him and woke him up, he fired off a shot right away. Of course, we gave him a good bawling out, but we had survived with no more than a fright. A few days before that an Obergefreiter had been killed by a shot in the stomach in exactly the same way. In the evening we took turns fetching food from the field kitchen. The baggage train was housed in a village (Bela). The weather was starting to get pretty chilly. There was occasional snowfall.

"On October 31st we were relieved. But soon – on November 2nd – we are on the march again, heading for our new assignment."

Members of 1st. company after the attack. (Author)

Graves of fallen Fallschirmjäger. (Author)

Casualties was very high in I./Rgt.3. (Author)

A last tribute to comrades. (Author)

4

Vyborgskaya

Initially, while the 1st Battalion was eliminating the Petrushino bridgehead, the III./Rgt.3 was fighting at the Vyborgskaya bridgehead. Later on when the 2nd Battalion, the 13th and 14th Company, as well as the staff of the 3rd Regiment, were relocated in order to relieve army troops, a real crisis developed. The 3rd Regiment only succeeding in coping with it at the cost of many casualties and by hurriedly bringing in the 1st Battalion from Petrushino, which had been taken. A report from the 3rd Regiment described the terrain as follows:

"Sloping towards the east bank of the Neva River with a bluff directly by the riverbank, undulating ground with several sand pits, almost without ground cover with the exception of a copse of birch trees directly next to the bluff, several hedges and groups of trees. The houses in the town of Vyborg have already been destroyed. The road runs parallel with the Neva; light railway tracks run from east to west down to a jetty on the Neva. The enemy territory west of the Neva is terraced; the town of Dubrovska has extensive factories and forest outside of the built-up area."

The main battle field of the Germans was generally flat and the terrain to the rear was a swampy forested area. That is why the command of the Regiment evaluated the terrain as being unfavourable for an effective defence.

In the meantime, the weather had changed. A brief muddy period suddenly gave way to snow and frost. The Russians adapted very quickly to the freezing temperatures and for the most part they were fighting in winter clothing, while the paratroopers were still wearing the same uniforms that they had on in Crete.

Along with the orders for the 1st Battalion to hand Petrushino over to an army unit and to relocate to Vyborgskaya, the Battalion's commander von der Heydte returned from the main casualty station where he had been provisionally recovering from wounds. During his absence *Oberleutnant* Knoche had acted in his stead and had at that point received the order to have the battalion move out. The route led through the typical coniferous forest, but suddenly emerged into open country surrounding a village. The village itself was located about one kilometre away from the route on a small hill. At the spot where the route re-entered the forest, it was blocked by a horse-drawn canon battery. Although the Battalion was given the order to halt, congestion built up. Of all times that was the moment when six Russian fighter-bombers appeared, immediately picked out the column then promptly began strafing it. All of the paratroopers jumped for cover. No more bombs fell. The fighter-bombers preferred to attack the village which was fortunate for the paratroopers, as they were able to continue on their way more or less unscathed. Directly behind the front, where the battalion was deposited, *Hauptmann* von der Heydte was already waiting to allocate the men to the sectors. The men from the 3rd Battalion were already there and were thus relieved to some extent. Close to the combat zone there was a coniferous forest with what were once tall trees. The men called it "Flanders forest", in memory of the formerly desolate tangle of tree stumps during the First World War. The ground here was completely ploughed up by artillery fire. The positions that the paratroopers took over were a provisional system of trenches, some of which were intact and some shot up. But it was necessary to hold the positions. The destroyed enemy tanks provided good cover that was quite popular. The paratroopers dug themselves into the earth under the tanks which served as effective protection against massive artillery and mortar bombardments. The German troops were astonished at the materiel the Russians brought over the Neva. Neither the Luftwaffe nor artillery was able to destroy the temporary bridge built to skim just over the surface of the water and used to bring in heavy materiel at night, including tanks.

For the German command top priority was combating the enemy tanks. That is why the paratroopers were granted fourteen days of special leave (after the unit was relieved) for overpowering a tank of up to thirty tons, and three weeks for tanks over thirty tons. In addition, they were instructed that having a tank "break through" was never a reason to surrender a position. The battle against the enemy infantry that was following them had to be fought with all the more tenacity.

The weapons the paratroopers dreaded most were what the troops called the "Ratsch-Bumm" (the 76.2mm field gun M1942, also called SiS-3), the 12cm mortar and the flamethrowers. It was discovered that the infantry attacks were frequently carried out with flamethrower support. The troops were also instructed to shoot those out first.

The Russian soldiers could be divided into two categories: active soldiers and civilians from Leningrad who were just dressed up in uniforms. They only had one thing in common – namely hunger, and both types hoped for loot. However, the tenacious defence of the paratroopers succeeded in preventing that. Because the enemy was only a few metres away, every night *Feldwebel* Scholz and *Oberjäger* Canzler, who both belonged to the 2nd Company and were both Sudeten Germans and able to speak Russian, tried to convince the hungry Russians to defect. In this way the 2nd Company lured over up to thirty defectors a day, most of them workers from Leningrad who had just been stuck into a uniform.

Nevertheless, the numbers of Russians seemed to be inexhaustible. The freezing temperatures were an additional problem, and the Neva and Lake Ladoga froze up. So the Russians were able to get new supplies in as well. When that happened, the defections suddenly stopped.

Red Army soldiers in outstanding condition and clothing, with excellent equipment and weapons, all of them in white camouflage shirts, suddenly materialised in position opposite the paratroopers. The Germans were issued something that was supposed to be winter clothing, but it mostly consisted of extra under-jackets, woollen gloves and a few pairs of felt boots so the sentries at least could be fitted out. By contrast, there was no lack of provisions and ammunition.

Obergefreiter Else remembers:

"So we set off, heading towards Vyborgskaya. There we were put under the control of several machine gun units and combat engineers. The trench positions of the Germans and Russians were only a few metres apart. I think it was about 100 metres. Before we took up our position, Feldwebel Rentsch divided our half-platoon into two groups. In addition, he allocated a bunker to us. Our first team consisted of Oberjäger Paul Lammoth as Gewehrführer, me as Schütze 1; Schütze 2 was Jäger Hein van Koll and Jäger Miesock was also one of us. We had to march quite a long way to get to the main battle line. At the first anti-aircraft artillery and machine gun emplacement, we entered the main battle line trench. Then we turned right towards the combat engineers. But right smack in the middle was the most dangerous section of the main battle line. It was never occupied – neither by the Russians nor by us – but everybody had to pass through it. That meant that when we were running through that section, we had to pull the pins on our hand grenades, throw them over into the Russian trench and keep going at a marching pace through the trench. When we had reached our machine gun position, two combat engineers always welcomed us. They were the left wing of a company of combat engineers. The combat engineers had their shelter approximately forty metres to the right of our sub-machine gun emplacement. The entire length of the anti-aircraft artillery, machine gun and combat engineer company was approximately 200 metres. Thank goodness nobody knew how thinly our troops

were spread out along that section of the front line. Our predecessors had fortified the sub-machine gun position quite well. There was a well-camouflaged observation lookout and on both sides there was a small bunker to the left and right of the sub-machine gun. A demolition charge and several rifles were already placed at the ready. Geographically speaking, the position was situated within a large curve of the Neva. Right in front of us there was a large island in the middle of the Neva.

"The Russians set up their final assembly point behind that island, on the other side of the river. They also launched attacks on us from there at night. There was a sturdy smokestack to the right, on the mainland behind the island. Several observers were posted on top and constantly kept an eye on us. Everybody fired at the smokestack – artillery, anti-aircraft and anti-tank guns – but nobody succeeded in bringing it down.

"The Russians were much better at hitting the pine trees behind us – in the Flanders forest. They toppled with loud crashing thuds when the Russian 'Ratsch-Bumm' guns hit the mark. But then it was time. In our position we already heard the clattering of the Russian tanks. We wondered how many of them there might be? Usually there were two or three tanks. One of them stopped behind the main Russian battle line, opposite our position, and observed us. Van Koll already had a demolition charge in his hand and was ready to jump up. But then the tank turned towards the left and headed for the position of the combat engineers. Just before it got there it stopped – but that was a big mistake. In the light of the signal rockets we watched as one of the combat engineers ran towards the tank with a demolition charge. He attached it to the tank and ran back right away. The tank was only able to continue on a zigzag course up to the combat engineer position, where it dug itself in until it got stuck. Then we captured the team manning the tank, and thus took our first prisoners.

"The emplacements of the artillery and the Nebelwerfer were right next to our bunker. We were not safe in that position either, because grenades kept battering the area as well. Then the Nebelwerfer responded. But we overshot the target by approximately 100 metres. Every time we thought the end of the world had come.

"As usual – in this situation van Koll improvised wherever he could. What he liked to do most was to pop over to the 4th Company to get fresh laundry. Our Spieß , Hauptfeldwebel Linke – was also pleased about that. He knew very well that van Koll was better at organising than he was, and that he was much more cunning. Once he stole a roast right out of a pan during an air attack when everyone else had run for cover. Then even the Spieß just shook his head. Hein van Koll never stole from necessity: it was a passion. But he always shared with all of us.

"Some snow had already fallen. It had taken on a dingy colour because of the numerous artillery hits. The Russians had dug trenches in their positions. We could see the heaps

of freshly turned earth. They were definitely planning an attack. The distance between us and the Russians was so small that we could almost look our opponents in the eye. Every once in a while we got a few defectors. The defectors were all clean and dressed properly. The first thing they said was always 'Germanski Brot!', meaning 'German bread'. They were all hungry.

"Finally, the day that we had been dreading for so long arrived. At ten o'clock in the morning a massive barrage of our section started. Nobody knew when the attack would begin. There was only one thing to be done. Run for cover and keep an eye on what was happening. The grenades and splinters kept crashing around us until three o'clock in the afternoon and each one of us was alone with his thoughts. Then our moment came. The Russian artillery ceased its fire along the entire line. For us that was the signal to grab our weapons and take aim at our opponents. The Russians slowly emerged from their trenches and advanced towards us. My heart almost sank to my boots. Hein van Koll calmly said: 'Oh, oh – they're coming. They're definitely not gentlemen, they're on their way and they intend to kill us!' The attackers rose up along the entire Russian position and confidently yelled: "Hurrah!". Thank goodness they were only coming towards us slowly. When they had got as close as about forty metres, grenades suddenly crashed into their positions. The entire attack force from their position ran for cover. That was their mistake. Nobody knew whether the grenades that were falling were Russian or German! My sub-machine gun stood to my right. It only shot brief volleys. I was not able to really remedy the mistake of the night attack of Petrushino. Van Koll and Miesock were standing up and firing as fast as they could. Only van Koll kept on making remarks: 'What's that guy got on his back? Is that somebody coming with a hand cart?' What he meant was a Russian sub-machine gun. The Russians were creeping and crawling forward towards our trench. The one closest to us stopped, lying just 4 metres away from our trench. Meanwhile van Koll even took the time to lit up a cigar. I found myself wondering whom he had stolen it from? At the end of the attack we had twenty-three defectors. They were all taken to the rear. When the attack was over, things quieted down and we were able to move around more freely again. Miesock and van Koll suddenly had a great idea. They thought the Russian trench must be empty by then. And they suggested that we should go over and take a look. I said: 'Don't you even dare do that! You must be crazy!' Shortly after midnight it happened. I saw the two of them, crawling on all fours through a flat trench that led to the other side. I took out my pistol and called out: 'Come back right away or I'll shoot you both!' They looked around and came back. After that the days went by as always, sentry duty in the position and resting in the bunker.

"Then suddenly we were told that the 4th Company was to assemble in a small cottage located far to the rear; we were spread out along all of the sections of the front and among all of the companies. So we got to see each other again, and while everyone was trickling back they were often heard to remark, 'Wow, you're still alive!' We were standing in front of the small cottage in the cold and snow until a superior officer said

to us, 'This little cottage will be your accommodation for tonight – go in and make yourselves comfortable. Tomorrow you will be moving to a new position.' There were thirty-two of us all told and all of us actually found a spot in the little house. The first row sat with their backs to the wall and their knees pulled up. The second row did the same – and so on. We were so dead tired that we soon fell asleep, and nobody's legs fell asleep.

"The next evening we got on two heavy transport vehicles and set off to the new position. This time it was a huge sand hollow in the Wespennest. The team on our heavy transport vehicle consisted of eighteen men who were deployed on the right wing. The positions were all along the edge of the sand hollow. The most valuable asset was the large fortified bunker on the right wing. But before we had reached our position, first of all we said hello to a few comrades from our company. Alois Schmidt and Gustel Milotzkie were standing – lonesome and forlorn – next to their sub-machine gun and said: 'What the ___, eighteen men as reinforcements?'

"Our sub-machine gun position was located on the edge of the depression close to the bunker. When we arrived, it was still dark. The hornets' nest was straightforward terrain, with undergrowth, fallen trees and many bushes. Suddenly Oberleutnant Straehler-Pohl (the commander of the 3rd Company) appeared with new orders. They specified: We were supposed to pretend to be a full position unit. Which meant throwing hand grenades like mad. First three men threw hand grenades and then four or five men etc. – always alternating the pattern and always from various positions. We kept up that alternating system along a 200 metre stretch. We were not able to see any of the enemy, but in exchange the Russians managed to hit the bull's eye on purpose a few times. One comrade, Grabmeier, was shot in the head and collapsed right into Fritz Barnet's arms. Hagemann flew out of the bunker when a grenade came down close to him. He turned on his own axis and fell forward. He was bandaged up provisionally in the bunker, but we never saw him again."

Gottfried Emrich was also there in Vyborgskaya:

"Dragging the weapons behind us while en route had us sweating buckets. We met many Russian women who were looking for meat. They butchered every dead horse right there on the spot. Only the skeletons were left lying on the road.

"At night we had to set up our new position. It was already getting dark. We were lying around, spread out and resting from the long march, when there was a grenade hit while we were eating. We rushed apart, one man staggered and fell. A fragment had slashed his carotid artery.

Obj. Gottfried Emrich experiences the first snow in Russia. (Emrich)

October 31, 1941, members of the 4. Kp. on the way to Wyborgskaja. From left to right: Obj. Walter Fontaine, ?, Obj. Gerhard Grützmann, Renner, ?, Company Chef Oblt. Adolf Peiser. Note the tactical symbol of 4.Kp. a heavy machine gun on a blue background with four-leaf clover. (Emrich)

Changing positions at the Newa. Obj. Emrich at right. (Emrich)

Tactical sign of I./Rgt.3. (Author)

Watching the enemy with a "Scherenfernrohr." (Author)

Terrain evaluation. (Author)

Paratroopers reinforcing positions. (Author Collection)

Deep snow in Vyborgskaya. (Author Collection)

MG position inside a bunker. (Author)

Stab Officer Oberleutnant Kurt Veth. (Author)

"After that we set up our new position. My signal corps was assigned to the mortar. There was snow everywhere. After the individual mortars were assigned their positions, we started moving into our bunker. We dug all night – we already got down pretty deep. On the next morning we started to collect logs. It was lucky for us that we found an abandoned bunker close to the small wood, sort of like a log cabin, with thick logs that we were able to use. It was a huge amount of work, because we had to drag the heavy logs all the way to our bunker and – in the course of that – we had to cross the clearing that was churned up by the shelling. In the early morning light I fell into a hole full of water: my feet got wet, my trousers froze.

"Gorski and I dragged lumber tirelessly. We were back at the log cabin, pulling out the logs one by one. Then suddenly – like a monster thundering and growling from far away – the thunder of shelling started up and we had to lie down, pressing ourselves into the ground. Fragments were everywhere; clods of earth were flying through the air. The impacts were spread out. The only thing we could imagine was that the firing was in preparation for a Russian attack. And they had picked out our sector. We already heard the Russians yelling "Hurrah!" from afar. They were coming, they were attacking! The barrage eased off a bit, but we were still forced to take cover. Individual rifles shots slashed through the air. We were still lying there, and none of us had taken a weapon along. We had left everything lying by the newly built bunker so as to be less encumbered when working. Then the calls of the Russians that we heard got quite loud: they were still hidden by the forest, but the shooting from rifles and machine guns was getting really loud. First of all, we definitely had to get back to our weapons. We ran back to our bunker across the clearing, dodging impacts. A company of engineers was brought forward for a counter-attack. The Russians were trying expand their position once again at the Vyborgskaya bridgehead.

"Wounded men came past us. The firing gradually stopped. Gorski refused to listen to our warnings: he jumped out of the bunker right away to get a few more boards. He got as far as the clearing, when a terrible barrage started up again as revenge for the failed attack. Dark clouds of gun smoke blanketed the ground, and our faces got black. It had only been a few minutes since Gorski left the bunker, when we heard gurgling calls for help. That could only be Gorski. Two men jumped out of the hole and dragged him back. With a pleading look in his eyes, Gorski whispered weakly, asking us to kill him. His body was completely shredded by iron, a bull's eye had wounded him horribly. Two men were instructed to take him to the casualty station. They laid him on a tent canvas and carried him away, his legs dangling loosely in his trousers. With one last look, I bid farewell to my last comrade from Meißen, Edmund Gorski, on November 3rd. I had lost a great comrade from my signal unit. He died on the way there. I did not even get to see his grave. When I got back to Germany later on, I wrote to his parents.

Jäger Edmund Gorski (4th company) killed on the Neva front. (Emrich)

Edmung Gorski wearing a Kanonier (gunner) uniform. (Emrich)

Fallschirmjäger near the frontline. (Author)

Fallschirmjäger foxholes near the Neva. (BA Koblenz 1011-548-0702-19)

Veth with an officer. Note the white painted helmet and the Luftwaffe Bergmütze (Mountain cap). (Author)

Watch duty. (BA Koblenz 1011-548-0723-15)

Heinz Glüsen with Obergefreiter Heinz Anders and Schäfer near their bunker. (BDF)

Russian village near the Neva. (Author)

4th company commander Adolf Peiser. (Author)

Oberjäger Wilhelm Baumann (4th Kp.) in Wyborgskaja. (BDF)

On the way to the field-kitchen. (BDF)

Paratrooper wearing a white net on his helmet. (Author)

Paratroopers wearing improvised camouflaged material. (private collection)

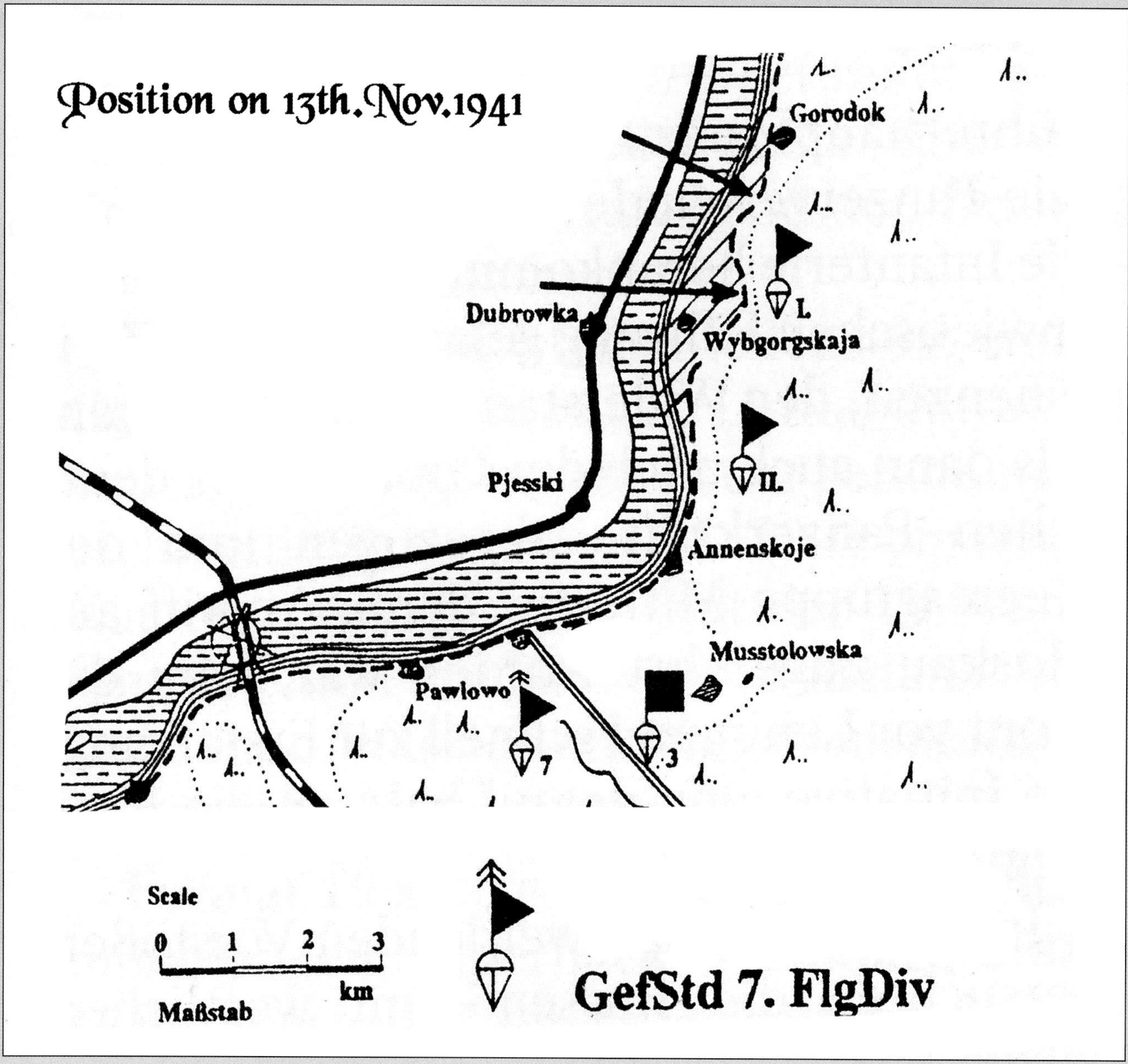
Position on 13th.Nov.1941
Gorodok
Dubrowka
Wybgorgskaja
I.
II.
Pjesski
Annenskoje
Musstolowska
Pawlowo
7
3
Scale
0 1 2 3
km
Maßstab
GefStd 7. FlgDiv

"The Russians had spotted our position and there was no doubt that they believed that we had heavy weapons in position there. There was no sense in staying there. Even the company commander agreed that we should change our position. When it got dark, we set up a line from the observation post to our mortar position and moved to the other position we had been ordered to, along with all of our equipment. There was a system of bunkers and positions spread out between a thin covering of trees. The mortar unit was setting up their grenade launchers. We – the platoon leader of the mortar unit, Jäger Müller (signal corps) and I – picked out a small bunker, three by three metres, for ourselves. I had built ourselves a stove out of a mortar ammunition case and we used it to cook on. Our favourite food, which we made quite often, was toasted bread: with butter or pork lard melted on it. But our stove had one disadvantage: our faces got all black from the soot.

"If we looked to the left over the edge of the trench, we could see the higher terrain where the Russians had dug themselves in. The front line of the Russians was only thirty metres away at the front near the rifle company, which was connected to us by a system of trenches. If we listened carefully we could clearly here Russian being spoken. Jäger Müller and I patrolled day and night looking for disruptions. On the second day after our change of position, we found out that an enemy squadron had bombed our previous position – so we were very lucky that we left it when we did. We were told that the only thing left was splinters of trees and ploughed up earth. In the meantime our company had suffered many deaths and casualties. Oberjäger Rohm, my "Gewehrführer", from Crete, Gefreiter Renner and Gefreiter Schmidt had been killed. One of the mortars that were allocated to a rifle squad had a barrel burst (three dead, one wounded). Death was our constant companion. The losses of the rifle companies were especially bad. Several times a day the Russians would try to thrust their way into our front. After massive artillery fire they would then attack and with the aid of tank support they were frequently successful and occupied part of our positions. Then every morning our companies would launch a counter-attack and push them back again. That was how things went on for quite a long time. Nerves of steel were needed. We could not rest any more; the light field cable was constantly being torn up. If a test message was not successful, we doggedly set off again, taking a field telephone, a grounding rod and a bag of tools. It was always a very dangerous undertaking – we never knew if we would be coming back.

"And so it went on – day and night. We felt our way along the communication line and were always pretty glad when we got back. The weather often meant there were snow drifts. Our ranks were getting emptier and emptier, and our forces on the front were getting pretty sparse. We needed reinforcements urgently. As far as hygiene was concerned, things were very primitive: washing was quite infrequent, but the snow helped us get rid of the worst of the dirt. Our stubble had already grown into sizeable full beards."

Oberleutnant Knoche describes the situation at Vyborgskaya:

"Our main battle line encircled the bridgehead in a large semicircle. It only had one flaw at the seam between the 1st Company and my company, the 2nd, which was where there was a deep sack-shaped salient. To make matters worse, there was even a ridge of terrain from where the enemy could observe our flank on the one hand and also launch its thrusts on the other. It goes without saying that the enemy had concentrated large numbers at this bulge on the front and fortified it well. Attempting to eliminate it would have been a seriously risky venture because of our complete lack of reserves. That is why I entrusted my Leutnant Krüger, who was capable and vigilant, with sentry duty at that dangerous location. Krüger kept the sack-like salient under constant fire from our 5cm mortar. In this way he inflicted substantial casualties on the enemy and for the time being he brought enemy movements and activities to a standstill. But "Ivan" also demonstrated his inventiveness in light of that sack-like constellation. He dug his way further and further into the sack-shaped salient using a deep system of trenches that reached out like fingers. In those trenches the Russians were unobserved and protected and were therefore able to assemble and burst forth at a suitable moment. That would have created an extremely ominous situation for us, because if they had succeeded in breaking through, the enemy would have been able to attack our position from the flank and overrun it."

Oberleutnant Knoche continues:

"So for us the task was not only to recognise that danger and to adapt to it, but to eliminate it. The sack-like salient had to be cut off, no matter what the cost! That was the unanimous opinion of everybody, starting with the commander and all the way down to the very last enlisted man. However, the unanswered question remained: Where would we get the strength to accomplish that? There were no reserves that could have tackled the undertaking – neither at the battalion nor the regiment, because at that time all of our forces were deployed and tied up directly along the main battle line.

"For Oberst Heidrich, who was a master tactician, that was an unacceptable situation – as he confessed to me during a visit – and he wanted to eliminate it as fast as possible, even at the cost of the frontline. As he was relying on a promise that he was to be sent new reinforcements to form an attack reserve, with a heavy heart he had sent all of the available forces into the endangered sectors of the main battle line in order to relieve the units that were struggling with their last ounce of strength. And the reserves that were promised? Well, they actually did exist. But they had to be deployed at another location along the front where a crisis suddenly developed. When 'General Winter' made his appearance, the general situation had fundamentally shifted in favour of the Russians.

"Finally, the alarming reports about to the sack-shaped salient that we were receiving (they came from 1st and 2nd Company) continued to bother Hauptmann von der Heydte. Then – in line with the motto of 'God helps those who help themselves' – he came to a decision that was just as daring as it was dangerous. After he together with Oberleutnant Hepkes (the commander of 1st Company) had listened to my opinion of the situation, he asked whether each of us could make an entire platoon available for an operation against the 'sack' without endangering the main battle line. Because of the urgent necessity, we agreed – as long as the undertaking (which was of course supposed to be carried out at night) did not require any unacceptable losses and if it were concluded by dawn of the next day. Our willingness to earmark one platoon with about thirty men for the undertaking has to be regarded in light of the fact that the companies only consisted of about fifty to sixty men. Hauptmann von der Heydte promised to create a small reserve from the staff and intelligence corps to make it available. In this way, we prepared for an operation that was supposed to not only eliminate an important part of the striking power of the Russians at that section of the front, but was also supposed to demonstrate how powerfully the German paratroopers were still able to strike."

For the operation *Oberleutnant* Hepke selected the platoon of *Leutnant* Hubert Abratis. *Leutnant* Krüger under *Oberleutnant* Knoche volunteered along with his platoon. But Knoche was not really certain: which means that he had suddenly gotten a bad feeling about the decision. That is why he chose the platoon of *Leutnant* Enke and ordered *Leutnant* Krüger to give up part of his platoon to supplement Enke's platoon. *Leutnant* Krüger had to stay at the command post and ensure that there was an adequate supply of weapons.

So the Abratis and Enke platoons were equipped so that each on its own formed a strong, extremely powerful, but nevertheless mobile assault party.

The attack plan was relatively simple. During the late hours of the evening – when the Russians would not be expecting any attack – the two assault groups planned to attack simultaneously from the right and left sides, pinching off the salient by cutting through the base of the "sack", establishing a protective line in front and then clearing out the salient – which would then effectively be a pocket – from behind. Night time attack operations are always extremely dangerous for the attackers because of the danger of friendly fire.

Fallschirmjäger in the snow. (BA Koblenz 1011-538-0347-29)

Deep trenches near the frontline. (BA Koblenz 183-B18616)

Trenches near the Neva (Author)

Running to the frontline in Wyborgskaya. (Author)

Paratroopers attacking. (BA Koblenz 183-B18616)

Oberleutnant Knoche looks back:

"The operation took 'Ivan' completely by surprise and went like clockwork. The enemy everywhere was startled and alarmed and wild, completely unsystematic gunfighting began. Within the pocket that had been created, the surprise and fear was so great that part of the enemy troops surrendered without any resistance, but the majority killed one another in the prevailing chaos that ensued. Quite a few of the prisoners confirmed that. But there was also no other way to explain the heaps of bodies that we found in the pocket, especially in the trenches."

Oberleutnant Knoche continues:

"Around three o'clock in the morning, after the pocket was pretty well captured, Abratis and his platoon were able to finish clearing it out completely on their own. I ordered Leutnant Enke and his men to follow me forward in order to establish a line of defence that we could protect as fast as possible, because I expected a massive counter attack to be launched at that location at dawn.

"I also moved forward in order to be able to give instructions to Enke, who was to follow soon. As machine gun fire was occasionally strafing the terrain again and there was a definite possibility of encountering Russian stragglers, I covered the distance by jumping from one fox hole to another. It was almost a rule of thumb that you expect to find dead Russians in each of those holes in the ground. When I had just jumped into another hole, something under me moved. In the hole a wounded Russian was crouching on top of two dead bodies and I had jumped right on top of him."

Oberleutnant Knoche continues:

"I was still thinking about what to do with the wounded Russian, who was just begging and groaning, when I suddenly heard the typical clicking sound of an ammunition box and at the same time I saw a line of marching Russians silhouetted against the sky. I was already thinking that the enemy had broken through somewhere or had snuck in from outside when I heard a German voice from the line of men. I discovered that it was the voice of Oberjäger Berndt, who was wounded and lying on a blanket – and being carried by two Russians. What the heck was going on? Well, the answer to the puzzle was simply that Leutnant Krüger, who was responsible for fresh supplies of ammunition, did not have enough people. Oberjäger Berndt had offered his services, saying: 'Sir, I'll do that with my Russians.' He had then loaded up the ammunitions with seven prisoners and set off in front of them. En route he was shot in the leg. Of course, then the Russians could have attacked the wounded man and freed themselves. But they did not do anything of the kind. On the contrary – they helped Oberjäger Berndt bandage his leg, they laid him on a blanket and attached it to a carrying pole which two men hoisted then on to their shoulders. Oberjäger Berndt was giving instructions for speed and direction from his position on the blanket.

"Up front at the entrance to a Russian bunker we had captured, I met a 'Feldwebel', from the 1st Company who was just allocating a position to a machine gunner. The Feldwebel was still informing me about his impressions and what he had seen when Leutnant Enke already reported back to me. Starting from that point, I laid out the location of the new main battle line together with the sergeant and Enke and gave orders for speeding up the fortification of the position. Then, while I was examining the terrain in more detail, I almost bumped into Leutnant Krüger. Quite astonished, I asked him what he was doing and he answered, 'Looking for my men'. He told me that he had received news that all of his men had fallen or were wounded – that Enke had used them as 'cannon fodder', as Krüger put it. Of course, that was all complete nonsense. But evidently a wounded man who was transported to the rear and was in shock had made some remarks, which were circulated as rumours that Krüger heard. Krüger's men would go through fire and water for him, and Krüger would do the same for them. Now Krüger had run towards the battle sector himself in a mad rush in order to check things out himself."

Oberleutnant Knoche adds:

"Krüger was upset – I tried to calm him down and reminded him that I had ordered him to stay at the command post and fulfil the duties I assigned to him. That made him even more suspicious and apparently he believed that I only wanted to placate him. He insisted in getting some information himself. I had never experienced Krüger showing the slightest sign of disobedience, mistrust or even rebelliousness. So his sudden obstinacy totally mystified me. But all my cajoling did not do any good. I had to get a bit nasty and unequivocally tell him to fulfil the orders he had been given. It was only then that he went back without a word. Towards the morning when I got back to my command post, Werner Krüger was not there – he had not returned at all. We only found him later when it got light. A Russian infantry projectile had hit him not very far from my command post. Shot in the head! Death must have been instantaneous.

"One disaster rarely happens on its own: my second officer – Leutnant Karl-Heinz Enke was also killed that night. Of all things, it happened in the bunker entrance where I had given him his instructions. Enke had sat down in the entrance with the sergeant from 1st Company in order to discuss additional details, when a Russian with a machine pistol rushed out of the bunker. He shot Enke and the sergeant dead on the spot and wounded another two men before the bullet of a third paratrooper brought him down. Not one of us would have thought that an enemy soldier might still be hiding in the captured bunker. When we took a closer look we discovered: he was a 'commissar'."

The paratroopers expected the great counter-attack to begin at dawn. But the Russians did nothing. The paratroopers were astonished but happy, for they ended up having an unexpected breather and were able to fortify their defensive positions "in peace and quiet." However, the breather was short-lived. The Russians started concentrating their attacks on the right wing of the encircling ring. As a result, the 3rd Company under *Oberleutnant* Straehler-Pohl became strongly involved in the main focus of the defensive fighting. The Russians pounded the right wing with heavy artillery fire for days. As a precautionary measure, the paratroopers were forced to move men from the left wing to the right. However, the encircling ring of paratroopers held fast until relieved, even though the number of fighting men was steadily dwindling.

Oberleutnant Knoche concludes:

"The trench strength of the companies dropped to between thirty to fifty men – but that only means trench strength! Yes, that was the term that we had to use for an organisation that only consisted of shifting personnel that had been trained and made fit for the most daring of undertakings. But there they were just lying around in the dugouts and letting themselves be bombed to death, instead of transforming frontline situations by means of daring sorties, which was what they usually did. Quite possibly the high command finally understood that as well. But when we were relieved, the Russian soil near Leningrad was blanketed with some of our best paratroopers."

Oberjäger Emrich remembers his final days in Russia:

"23.11.: Regiment roll call: Our regiment commander, Oberst Heidrich, appeared before the regiment, which had dwindled down to just a really small bunch. His words were full of grief. Tears were running from the eyes of that man, who was so feared but also loved by his officers and men. He could always be found where the front was. It was the same with my battalion commander Hauptmann von der Heydte, who always stayed with his troops even though he was wounded several times. Those officers enjoyed great respect, and they were very much loved by their men and everybody went through fire and water for them.

"The regiment commander concluded his address with the following sentence: 'You are no longer just my soldiers, you are all my boys!' After that, officers and riflemen were awarded their decorations by the battalion commander, including Jäger Müller, who had patched the communication line with me so often – he received the Iron Cross 2nd Class. Many were awarded the Iron Cross 1st Class, while the others ended up empty handed. But at this point it should be pointed out: we did not do anything for the sake of decorations: we had only done our duty as soldiers."

Here are the last memories of *Obergefreiter* Friedrich Else:

"When we arrived in Wolfenbüttel, we assembled to march into our garrison – the homecoming 1st Battalion 3rd Regiment!

"There were only forty-two men left in our 4th Company. On the way to the barracks an innkeeper from Wolfenbüttel was standing by the roadside. As he knew many of my comrades, he wanted to watch us marching in and called out: 'Hey you guys, what company is this? It's pretty confusing.' On hearing that a jäger answered: 'Just shut up – this is our battalion!'"

Russian prisoner. (BA Freiburg)

Paratroopers in Wyborgskaja. (Author)

Oblt. Veth and Hauptmann von der Heydte in Wyborgskaja. The stress of combat is painted on their faces. (Author)

Awards for the Fallschirmjäger. Here Hauptmann von der Heydte. (Author)

Von der Heydte awarding paratroopers with the Iron Cross of 2nd Class. (Author)

An officer awarding paratroopers. (Author)

A survivor who earned the EK.2. (Author)

Mortar crew of 4th Company in Wyborgskaja. (Emrich)

Major Karl Lothar Schulz, Commander of III./Rgt.1, visiting the Stab. (Author)

Some of the rest of the 4.Kp. From left to the right: Meinz, Steinmann, Fischer, Müller, Fontaine, Emrich, Motas. (Emrich)

Jäger Müller earned the Iron Cross 2nd Class for his work as a string puller. Behind him Obergefreiter Fontaine. (Emrich)

Happy members of the 4th Company as they anticipate being home soon. (Emrich)

Evacuation of wounded and sick paratroopers. (Author)

Relaxation after the fight. Veth after a sauna. (Author)

Regiment Commander General Richard Heidrich. (Author)

On the way home. (Author)

5
Portraits and Documents

This page and opposite: Dr. Johannes Haß. (Author)

Paymaster Hans Hammermann was born in Burhave on September 24, 1914 (Lower Saxony). (Author)

Wilhelm Peters (3rd Company).

Walter Hess 3rd Kp. was killed at the Neva (Eric Queen)

At left is platoon leader Gottlieb Möck (4th Kp.), and at right Feldwebel Wilhelm Peters (both here with Feldwebel tabs). (Eric Queen)

Right: Hauptmann Franz Stangenberg. (BA Freiburg)

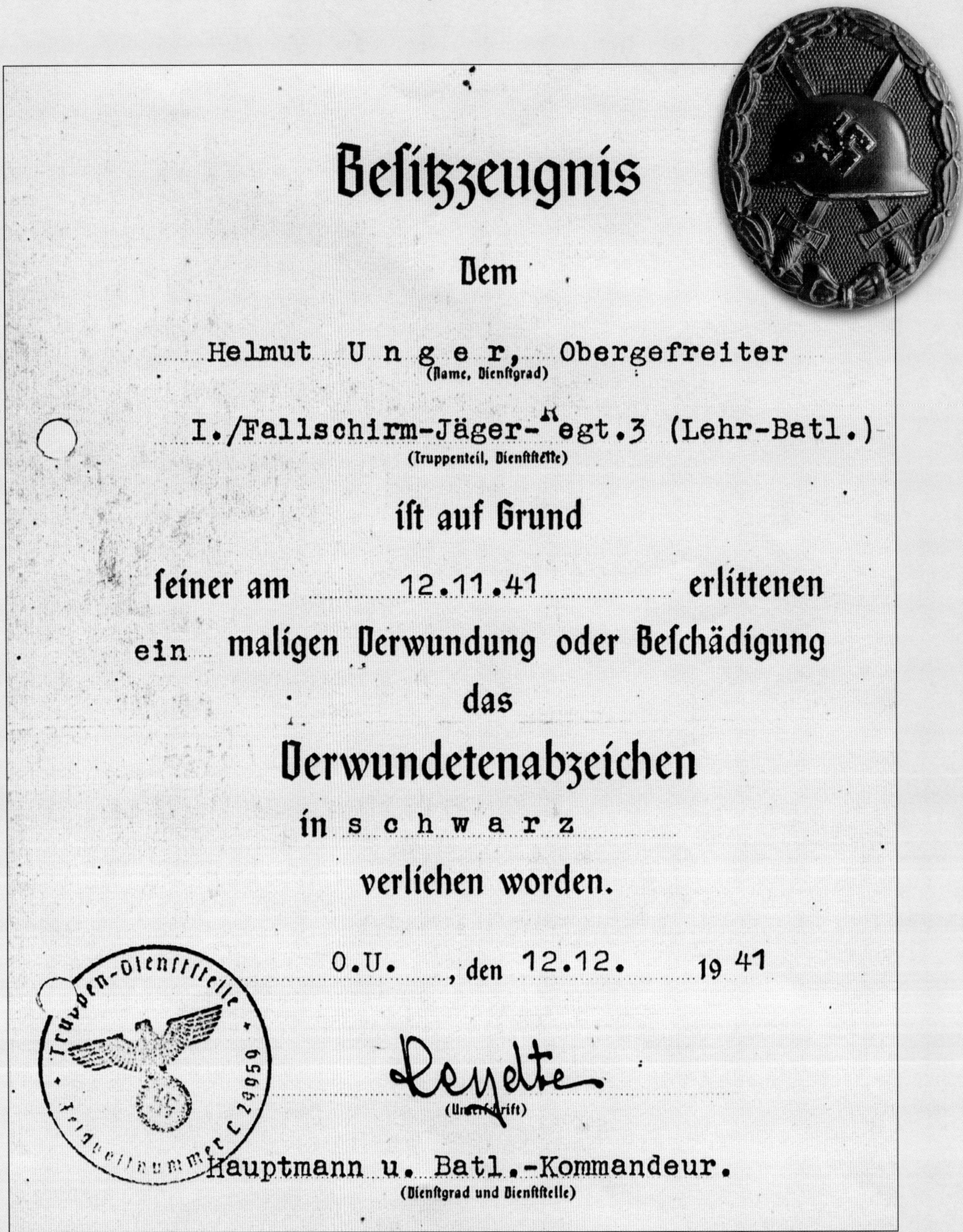

Besitzzeugnis

Dem

Helmut U n g e r, Obergefreiter
(Name, Dienstgrad)

I./Fallschirm-Jäger-Regt.3 (Lehr-Batl.)
(Truppenteil, Dienststelle)

ist auf Grund

seiner am 12.11.41 erlittenen

ein maligen Verwundung oder Beschädigung

das

Verwundetenabzeichen

in s c h w a r z

verliehen worden.

O.U., den 12.12. 1941

Heydte
(Unterschrift)

Hauptmann u. Batl.-Kommandeur.
(Dienstgrad und Dienststelle)

Truppen-Dienststelle • Feldpostnummer L 24959

Wound Badge in Black document of Obergefreiter Helmut Unger (3rd company). Note the unit "Lehr-Battalion" and von der Heydte's signature. Inset: The Wound Badge in Black worn by Helmut Unger. (Author)

Besitzzeugnis

Dem

Fritz Rentsch, Fw.
(Name, Dienstgrad)

I./ Fallschirm Jäger Regt.3 Lehr Batl.
(Truppenteil, Dienststelle)

ist auf Grund

seiner am 13.11.41 erlittenen

ein maligen Verwundung oder Beschädigung

das

Verwundetenabzeichen

in Schwarz

verliehen worden.

O.U., den 13.12. 1941

Truppen-Dienststelle
Feldpostnummer L 29950

Heydte
(Unterschrift)

Hauptmann u. Batl. Kdr.
(Dienstgrad und Dienststelle)

Another wound badge document this time of Feldwebel Fritz Rentsch member of 3rd company. (Chris Mason) Inset: Portrait photo of Rentsch. (Eric Queen)

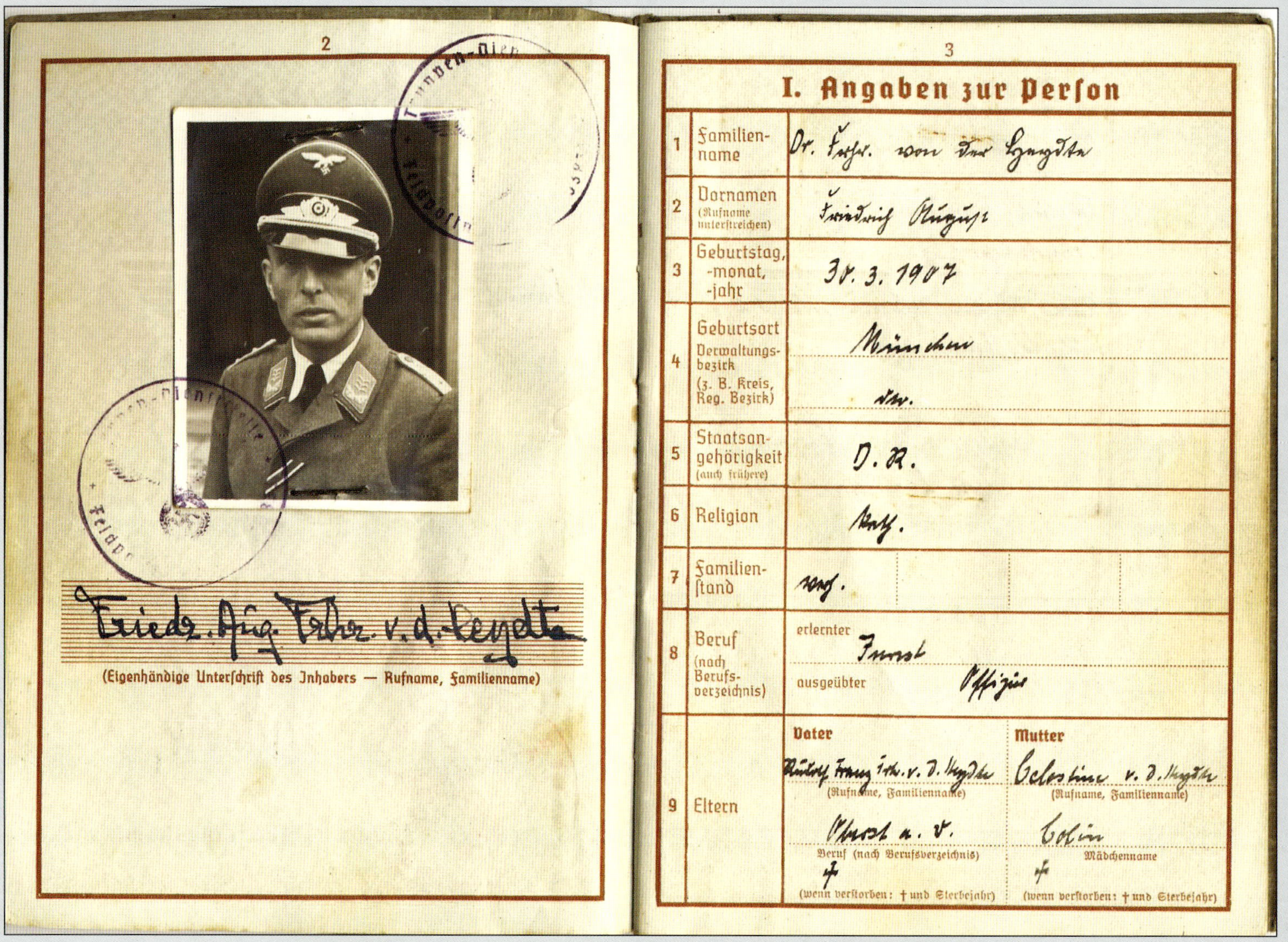
2

Friedr. Aug. Frhr. v. d. Heydte

(Eigenhändige Unterschrift des Inhabers — Rufname, Familienname)

3

I. Angaben zur Person

1	Familienname	Dr. Frhr. von der Heydte
2	Vornamen (Rufname unterstreichen)	Friedrich August
3	Geburtstag, -monat, -jahr	30. 3. 1907
4	Geburtsort Verwaltungsbezirk (z. B. Kreis, Reg. Bezirk)	München
5	Staatsangehörigkeit (auch frühere)	D. R.
6	Religion	Kath.
7	Familienstand	
8	Beruf (nach Berufsverzeichnis)	erlernter: Jurist; ausgeübter: Offizier
9	Eltern	Vater: (Rufname, Familienname); Beruf (nach Berufsverzeichnis); † (wenn verstorben: † und Sterbejahr) — Mutter: Celestine v. d. Heydte (Rufname, Familienname); Mädchenname; † (wenn verstorben: † und Sterbejahr)

Rare Wehrpass of Battalion commander Hauptmann von der Heydte with his details: name, date of birth, place of birth etc. (Private Collection)

Opposite

Top: Active service page. Note the entry I./Rgt.3. (Private Collection)

Bottom: Complete list of all of von der Heydte's combat actions. Note the entry for in Leningrad and the unit "Lehrbataillon." (Private Collection)

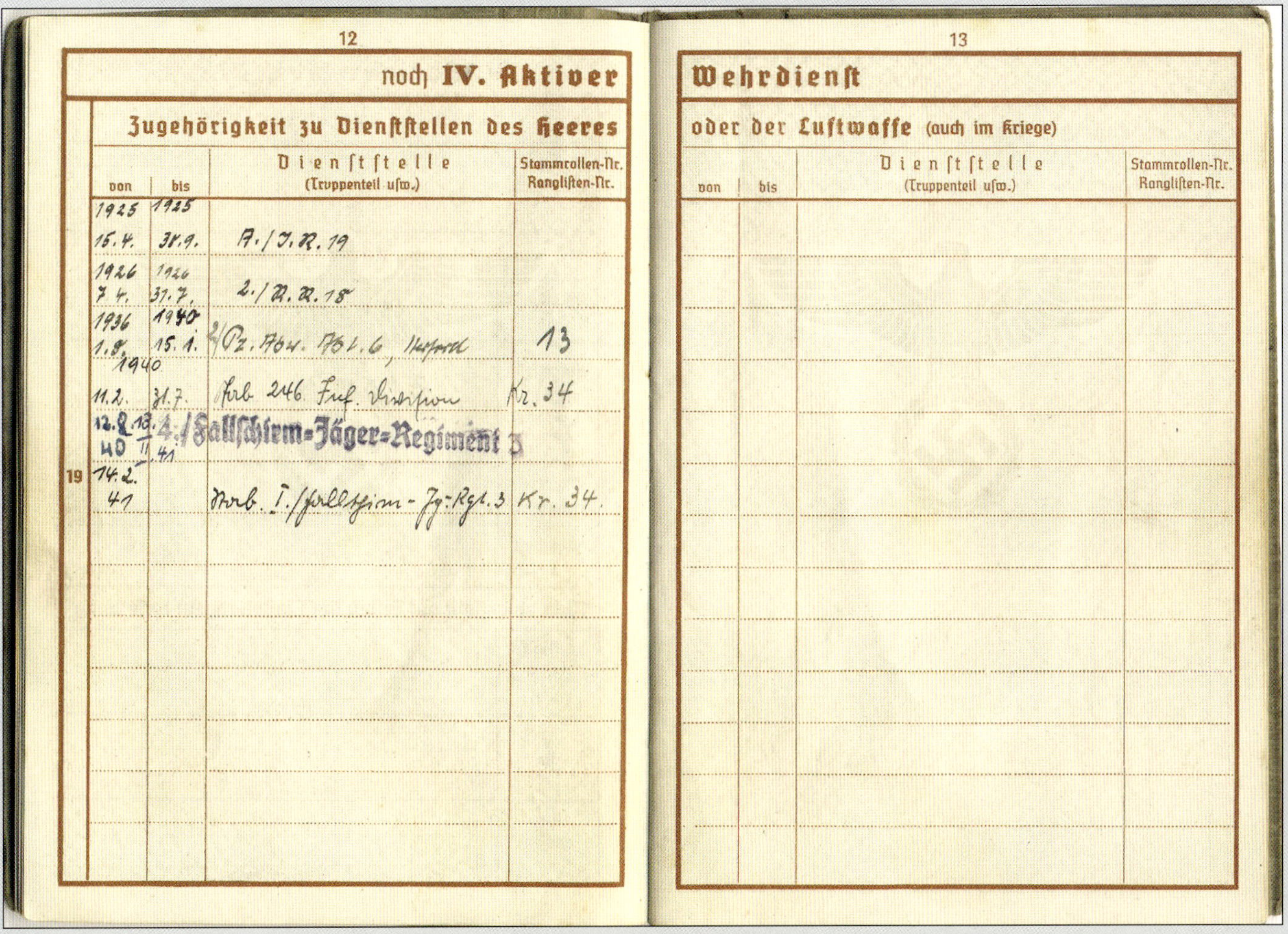

12

noch IV. Aktiver

Zugehörigkeit zu Dienststellen des Heeres

von	bis	Dienststelle (Truppenteil usw.)	Stammrollen-Nr. Ranglisten-Nr.
1925 15.4.	1925 31.9.	4./I.R. 19	
1926 7.4.	1926 31.7.	2./R.R. 18	
1936 1.8.	1940 15.1.	Pz. Abw. Abt. 6, Herford	13
1940 11.2.	31.7.	Stab 246 Inf. Division	Kr. 34
12.8. 40	13. 11. 41	4./Fallschirm-Jäger-Regiment 3	
19 14.2. 41		Stab I./Fallschirm-Jg.-Rgt. 3	Kr. 34

13

Wehrdienst

oder der Luftwaffe (auch im Kriege)

von	bis	Dienststelle (Truppenteil usw.)	Stammrollen-Nr. Ranglisten-Nr.

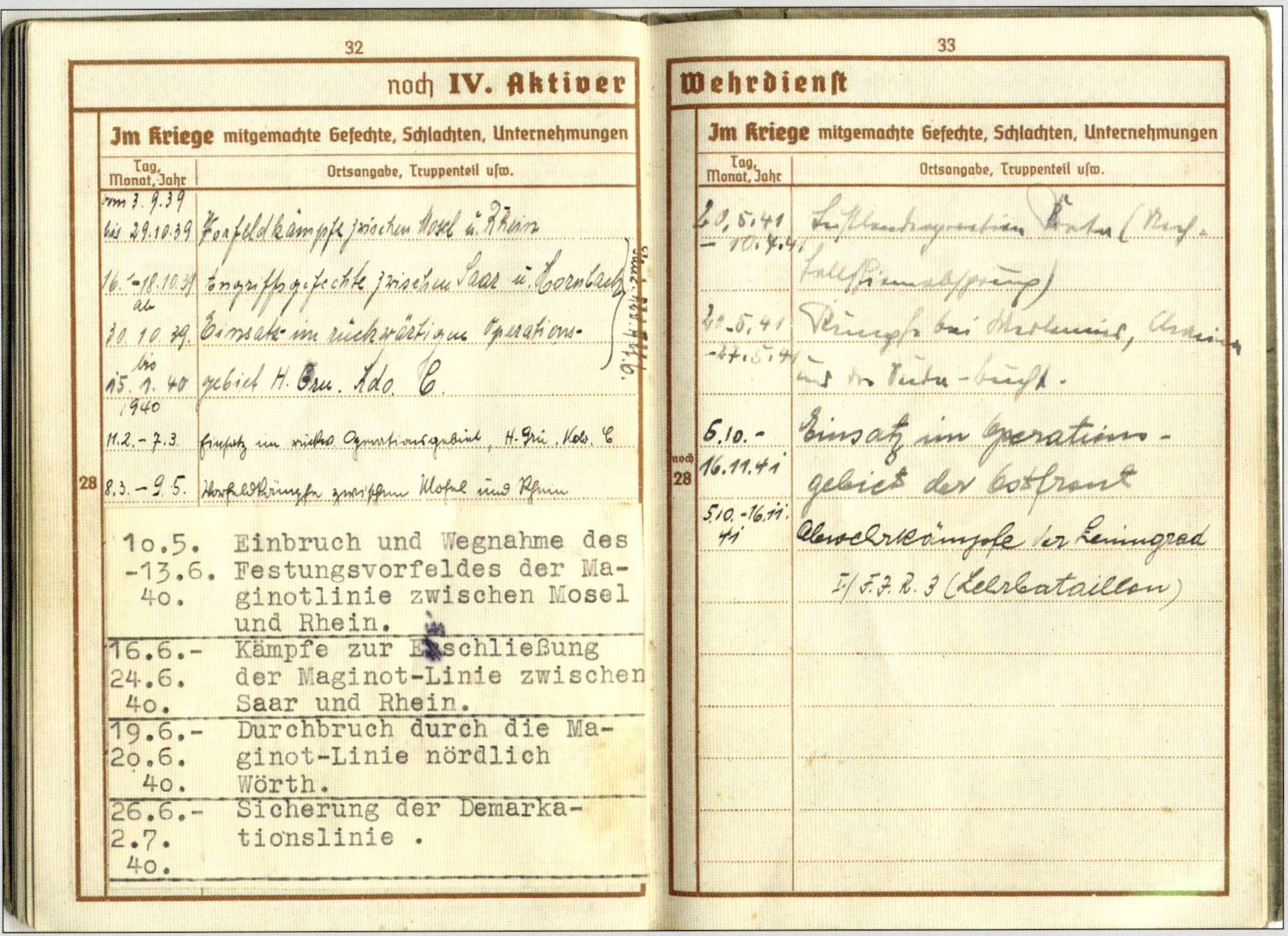

32

noch IV. Aktiver

Im Kriege mitgemachte Gefechte, Schlachten, Unternehmungen

Tag, Monat, Jahr	Ortsangabe, Truppenteil usw.
vom 3.9.39 bis 29.10.39	Vorfeldkämpfe zwischen Mosel u. Rhein
16.–18.10.39	Angriffsgefechte zwischen Saar u. Hornbach
ab 30.10.39 bis 15.1.40	Einsatz im rückwärtigen Operationsgebiet H. Gru. Kdo. C.
1940 11.2.–7.3.	Einsatz im rückw. Operationsgebiet, H.Gru. Kdo. C
28 8.3.–9.5.	Vorfeldkämpfe zwischen Mosel und Rhein
1o.5.–13.6. 4o.	Einbruch und Wegnahme des Festungsvorfeldes der Maginotlinie zwischen Mosel und Rhein.
16.6.–24.6. 4o.	Kämpfe zur Einschließung der Maginot-Linie zwischen Saar und Rhein.
19.6.–2o.6. 4o.	Durchbruch durch die Maginot-Linie nördlich Wörth.
26.6.–2.7. 4o.	Sicherung der Demarkationslinie .

33

Wehrdienst

Im Kriege mitgemachte Gefechte, Schlachten, Unternehmungen

Tag, Monat, Jahr	Ortsangabe, Truppenteil usw.
20.5.41 – 10.6.41	Luftlandeoperation Kreta (Fallschirmabsprung)
20.5.41 – 1.6.41	Kämpfe bei Malemes, Chania und der Suda-Bucht.
noch 28 6.10.–16.11.41	Einsatz im Operationsgebiet der Ostfront
5.10.–16.11.41	Newakämpfe bei Leningrad I./F.J.R. 3 (Lehrbataillon)

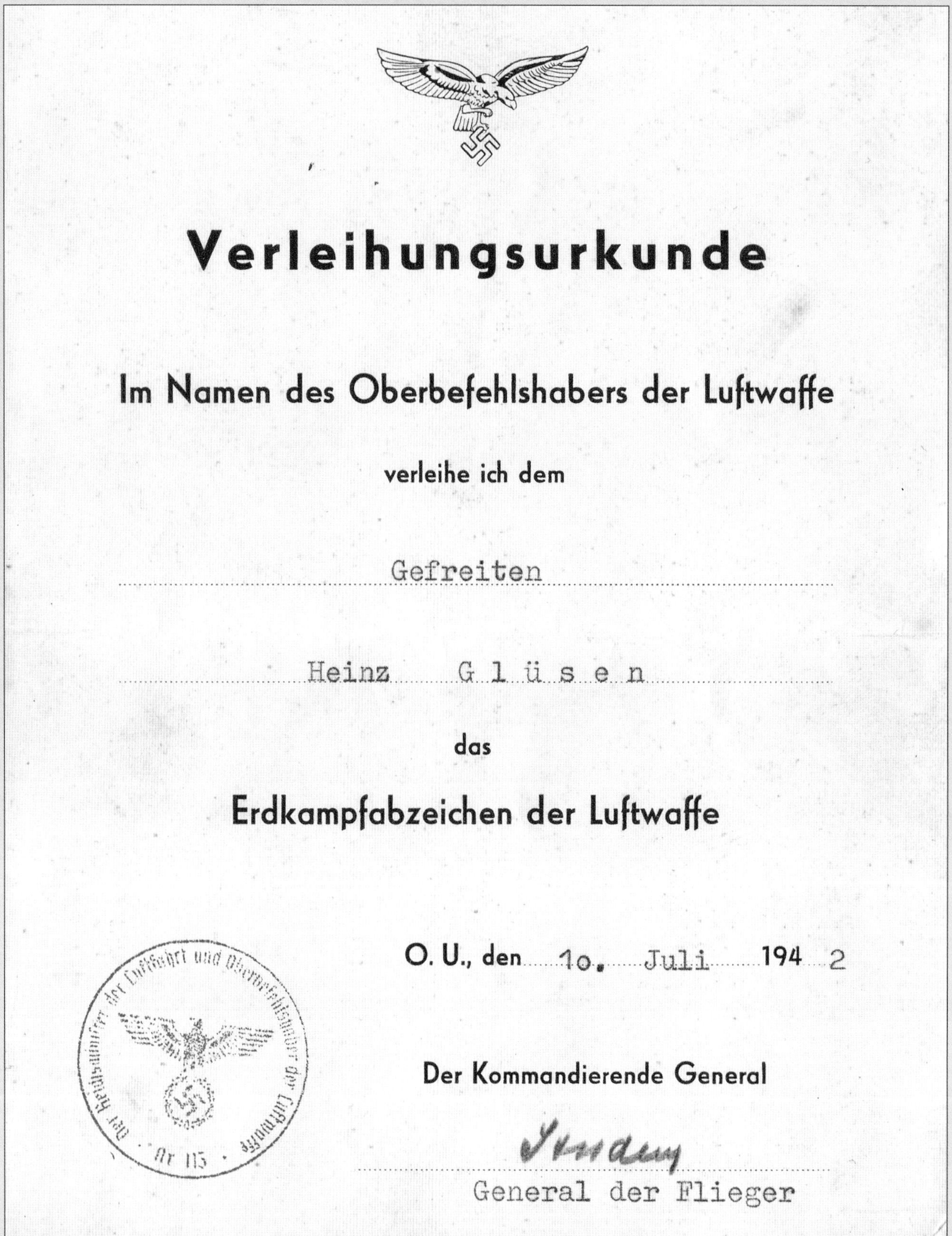

Verleihungsurkunde

Im Namen des Oberbefehlshabers der Luftwaffe

verleihe ich dem

Gefreiten

Heinz G l ü s e n

das

Erdkampfabzeichen der Luftwaffe

O. U., den 10. Juli **194** 2

Der Kommandierende General

General der Flieger

Der Reichsminister der Luftfahrt und Oberbefehlshaber der Luftwaffe · Nr 115 ·

9543 Maximilian-Verlag, Berlin SW 68, Ritterstr. 33.

Ground Assault document of Gefreiten Heinz Glüsen. (BDF)

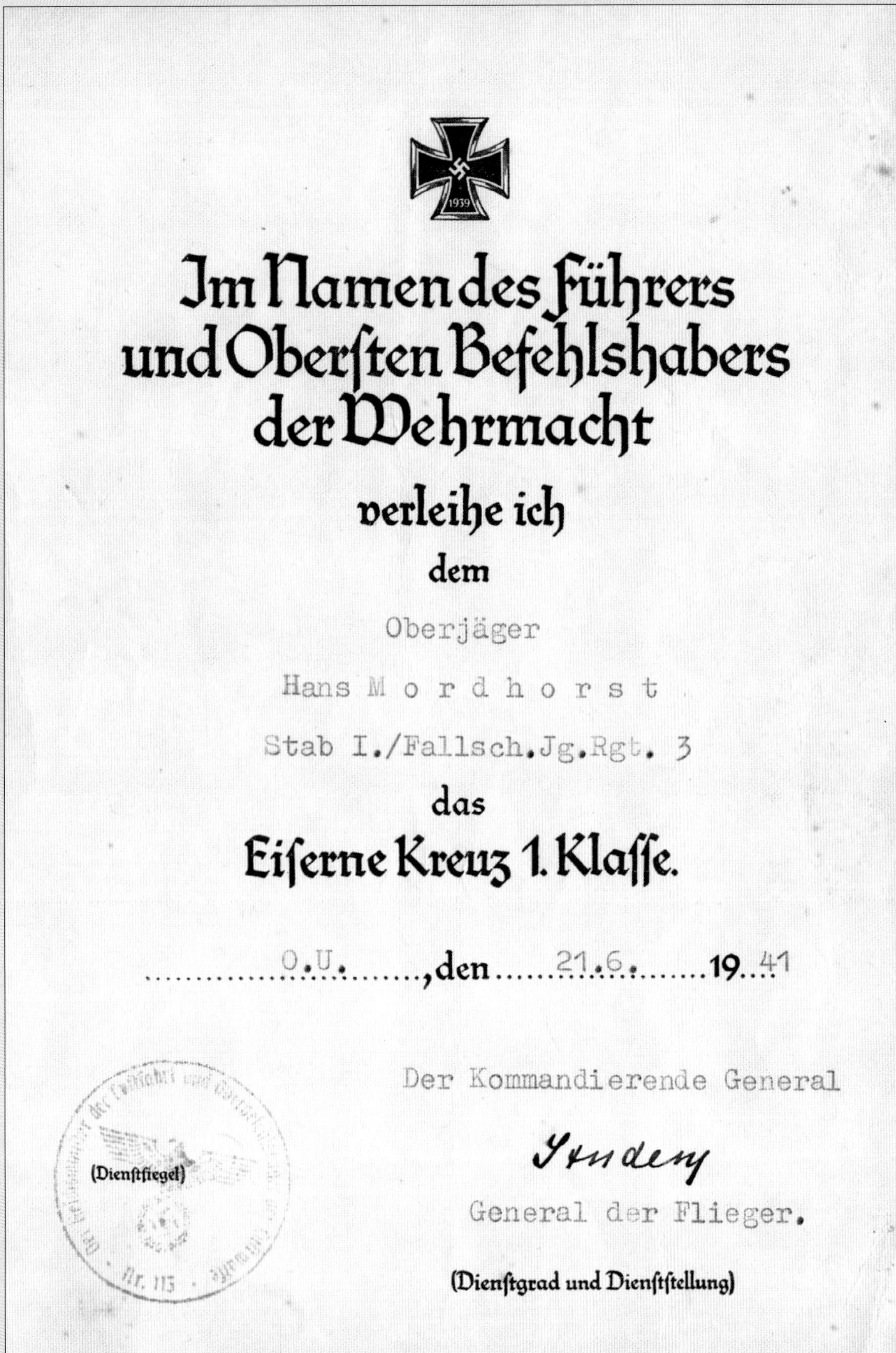

Im Namen des Führers und Obersten Befehlshabers der Wehrmacht

verleihe ich

dem

Oberjäger

Hans M o r d h o r s t

Stab I./Fallsch.Jg.Rgt. 3

das

Eiserne Kreuz 1. Klasse.

.........O.U. ...., den ....21.6. ....19..41

Der Kommandierende General

(Dienstsiegel)

General der Flieger.

(Dienstgrad und Dienststellung)

Iron Cross first Class for Oberjäger Hans Mordhorst I./Rgt.3. (Author)

Besitzzeugnis

Dem

Hans Mordhorst , Oberjäger
(Name, Dienstgrad)

I./Fallschirm-Jäger-Regt.3 (Lehr-Batl.)
(Truppenteil, Dienststelle)

ist auf Grund

seiner am 20.5.1941 erlittenen

ein maligen Verwundung oder Beschädigung

das

Verwundetenabzeichen

in schwarz

verliehen worden.

O.U. , den 26.7. 1941.

Truppen-Dienststelle
Feldpostnummer C 29959

Heydte
(Unterschrift)

Hauptmann u. Batl.-Kommandeur
(Dienstgrad und Dienststelle)

Mordhorst's wound badge document. Note von der Heydte's signature and the unit "Lehr Btl." (Author)

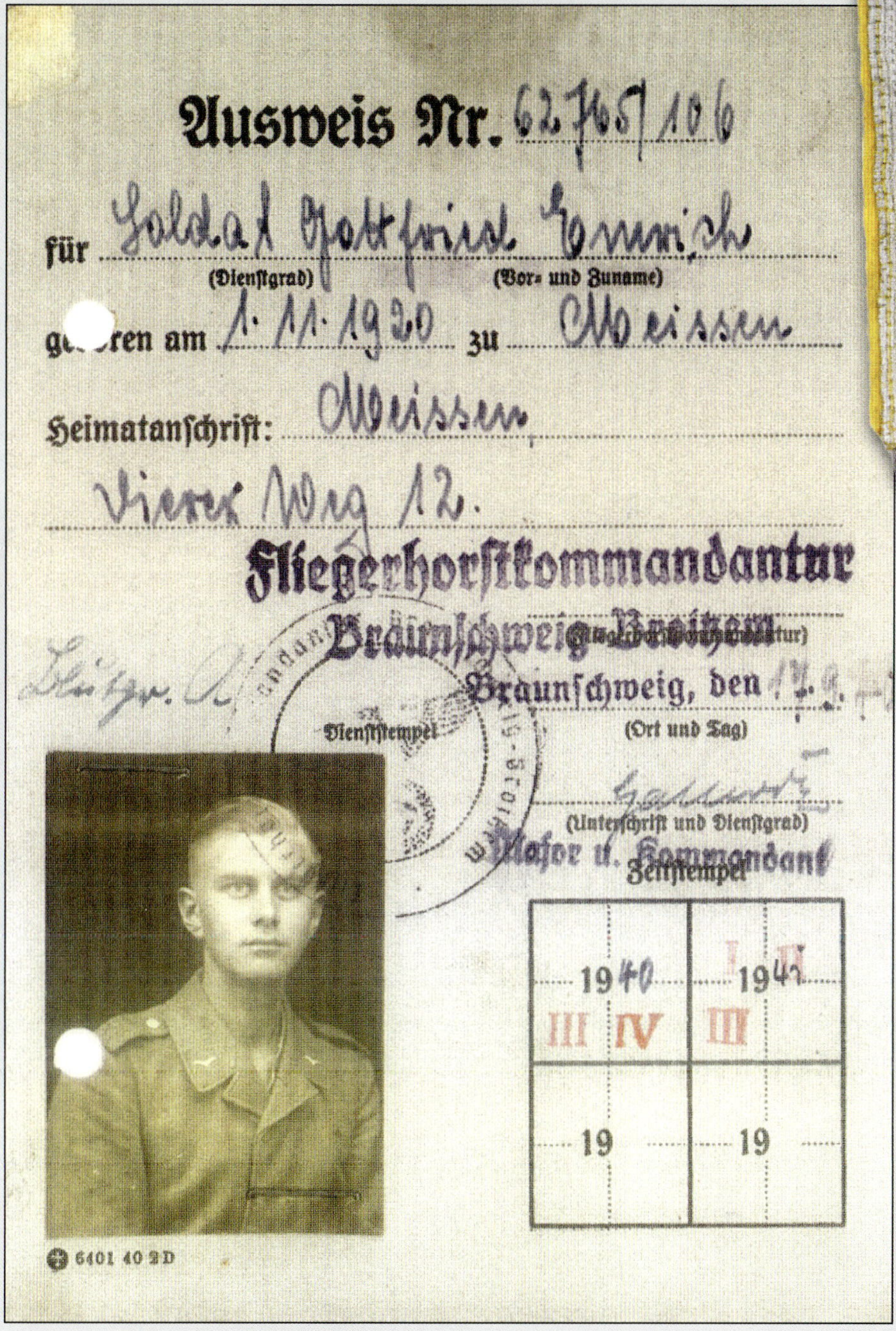

Ausweis Nr. 62/J65/106

für Soldat Gottfried Emrich
(Dienstgrad) (Vor- und Zuname)

geboren am 1.11.1920 zu Meissen

Heimatanschrift: Meissen,
Vierer Weg 12.

Fliegerhorstkommandantur
Braunschweig-Broitzem
(... Kommandantur)

Braunschweig, den 17.9.4[illegible]

Dienststempel (Ort und Tag)

(Unterschrift und Dienstgrad)
Major u. Kommandant

Zeitstempel

1940	1941
III IV	I II III
19	19

6401 40 2D

ID document of Gottfried Emrich. (Emrich)
Inset: Shoulder strap used by Emrich at the Neva. (Emrich)

6

Major Kurt Veth Grouping

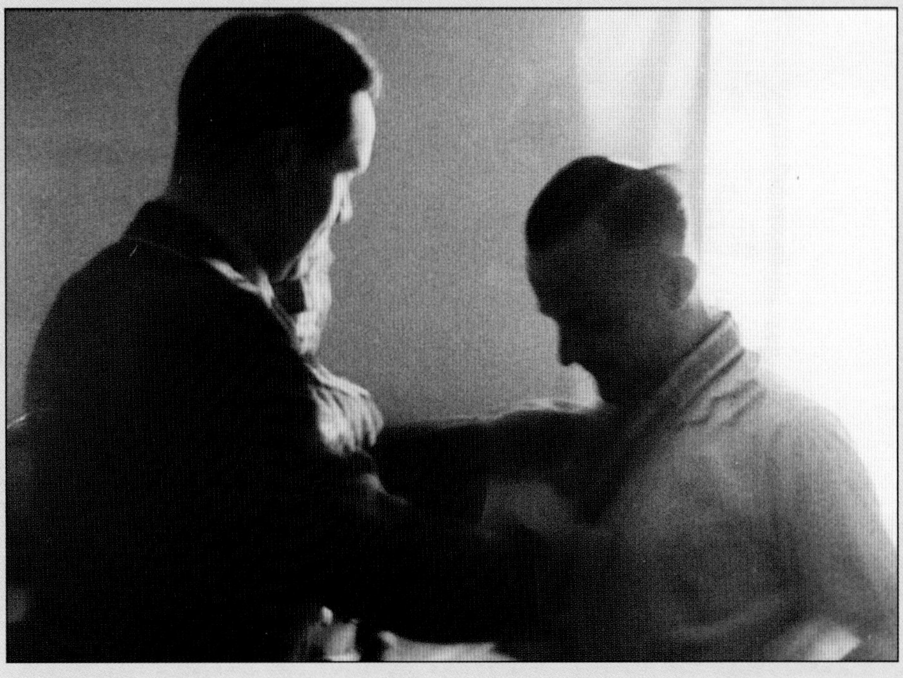

This page and opposite: Oberleutnant Veth received the Knight's Cross on September 30, 1944 as Hauptmann of the 1. Fallschirm-Jäger Division. Oberleutnant Veth distinguished himself during the battles in Italy. (Author)

The original Knight's Cross with Oak Leaves of Kurt Veth. (Author)

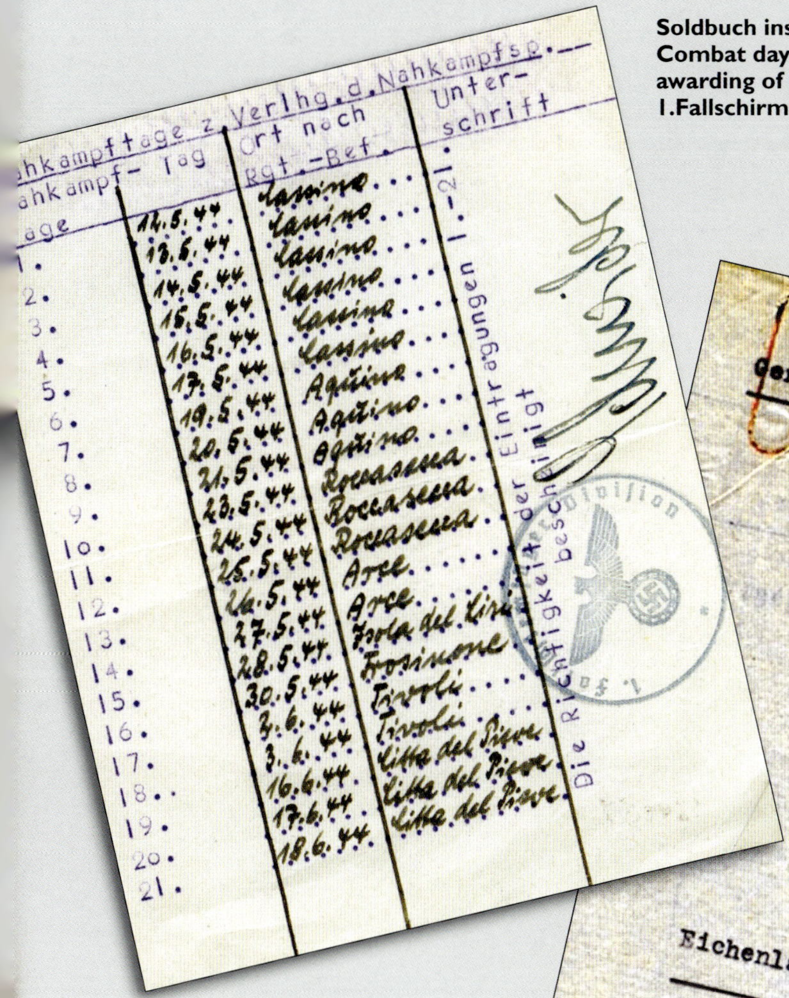

Nahkampftage z. Verlhg. d. Nahkampfsp.

Nahkampf-Tage	Tag	Ort nach Rgt.-Bef.	Unterschrift
1.	12.5.44	Cassino	
2.	13.5.44	Cassino	
3.	14.5.44	Cassino	
4.	15.5.44	Cassino	
5.	16.5.44	Cassino	
6.	17.5.44	Aquino	
7.	19.5.44	Aquino	
8.	20.5.44	Aquino	
9.	21.5.44	Roccasecca	
10.	23.5.44	Roccasecca	
11.	24.5.44	Roccasecca	
12.	25.5.44	Arce	
13.	26.5.44	Arce	
14.	27.5.44	Isola del Liri	
15.	28.5.44	Frosinone	
16.	30.5.44	Tivoli	
17.	2.6.44	Tivoli	
18.	3.6.44	Citta del Pieve	
19.	16.6.44	Citta del Pieve	
20.	17.6.44	Citta del Pieve	
21.	18.6.44		

Die Richtigkeit der Eintragungen 1.–21. bescheinigt

Soldbuch insert which captures a summary of Close Combat days (notice the Cassino entries) and confirms the awarding of the Close Combat clasp. Note stempel from 1.Fallschirm Division." (Author)

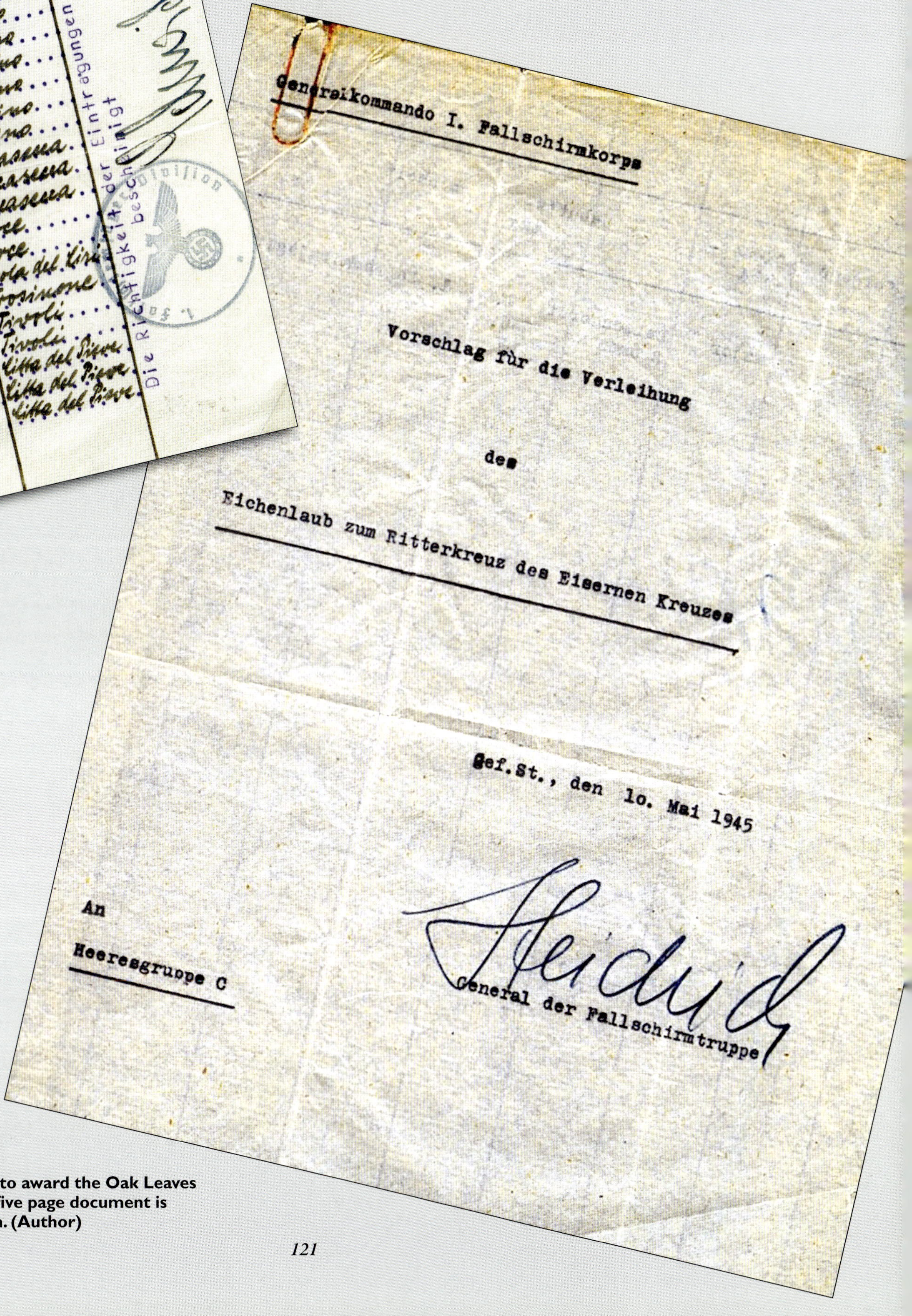

Generalkommando I. Fallschirmkorps

Vorschlag für die Verleihung

des

Eichenlaub zum Ritterkreuz des Eisernen Kreuzes

Gef.St., den 10. Mai 1945

An

Heeresgruppe C

General der Fallschirmtruppe

Original recommendation to award the Oak Leaves to the Knight's Cross. The five page document is signed by General Heidrich. (Author)

Auszugsweise Abschrift

Generalkommando I.Fallschirmkorps H. Qu.,den 30. 4. 1945

Der Kommandierende General

Am Ende des groessten Krieges aller Zeiten halte ich es als Kommandierender General fuer meine Pflicht, meiner Truppe ihre verdienten Auszeichnungen zu geben.

Ich verleihe deshalb, durch das Fehlen jeglicher Verbindung mit dem Luftwaffen-Personalamt, vorbehaltlich der nachtraeglichen Genehmigung des Oberbefehlshaber der Luftwaffe,

Nachstehende Auszeichnungen:

Das Eichenlaub zum Ritterkreuz des Eisernen Kreuzes

an

Major V e t h, Kurt 1. Fallsch. Jg. Division

Hauptquartier I.Fallschirmkorps, 30.4.1945

Als derzeitig hoechster Befehlshaber der unterstellten Verbaende.

In Vertretung des Oberbefehlshabers der Luftwaffe.

Der Kommandierende General des I.Fallschirmkorps

gez. H e i d r i c h

General der Fallschirmtruppe

F. d. R. d. A.

Oberst i. G.

Letter penned by General Heidrich informing Veth of the bestowal of the Oak Leaves. (Author)

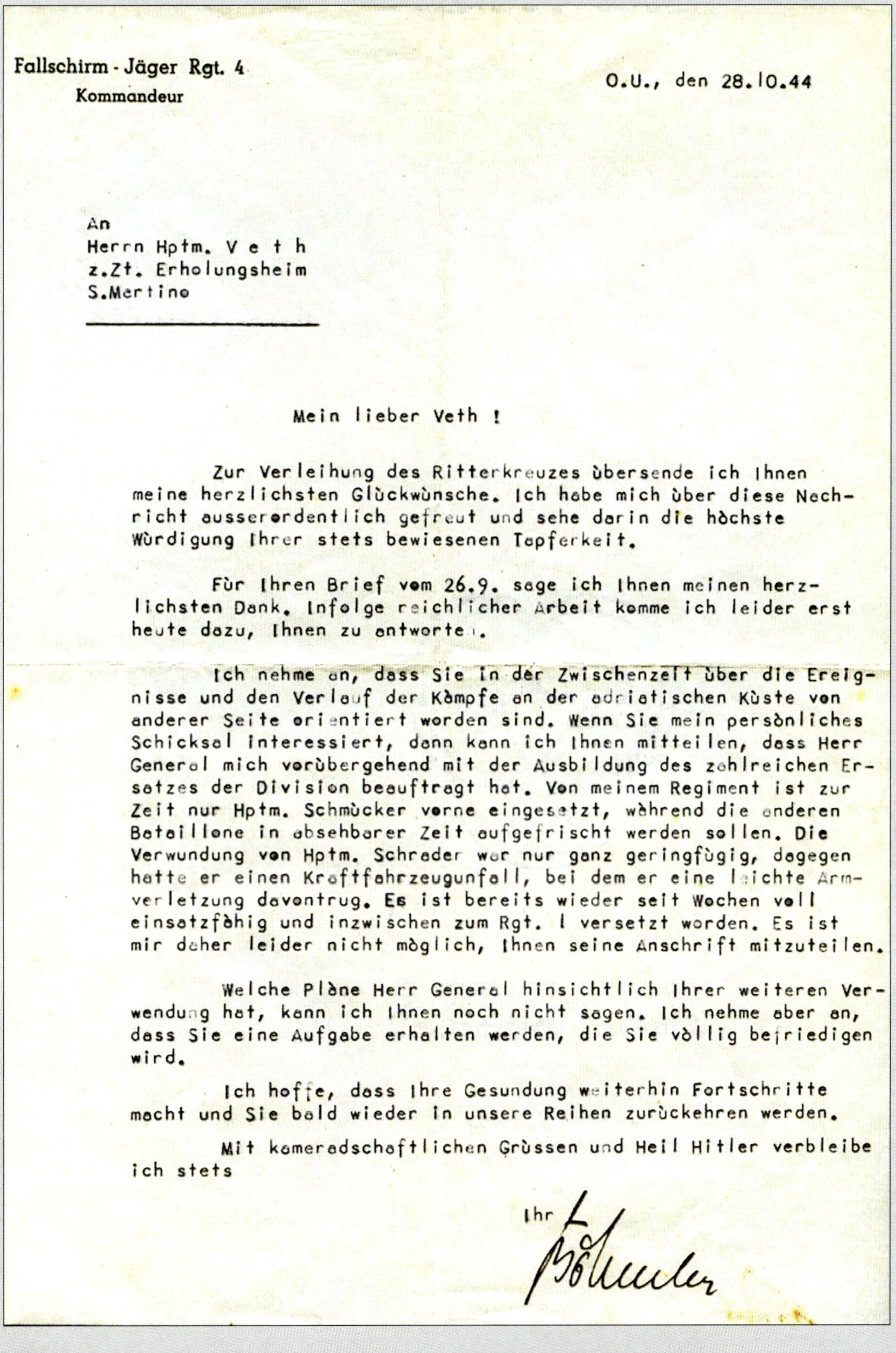

Fallschirm - Jäger Rgt. 4
Kommandeur

O.U., den 28.10.44

An
Herrn Hptm. V e t h
z.Zt. Erholungsheim
S.Mertino

Mein lieber Veth !

Zur Verleihung des Ritterkreuzes übersende ich Ihnen meine herzlichsten Glückwünsche. Ich habe mich über diese Nachricht ausserordentlich gefreut und sehe darin die höchste Würdigung Ihrer stets bewiesenen Tapferkeit.

Für Ihren Brief vom 26.9. sage ich Ihnen meinen herzlichsten Dank. Infolge reichlicher Arbeit komme ich leider erst heute dazu, Ihnen zu antworten.

Ich nehme an, dass Sie in der Zwischenzeit über die Ereignisse und den Verlauf der Kämpfe an der adriatischen Küste von anderer Seite orientiert worden sind. Wenn Sie mein persönliches Schicksal interessiert, dann kann ich Ihnen mitteilen, dass Herr General mich vorübergehend mit der Ausbildung des zahlreichen Ersatzes der Division beauftragt hat. Von meinem Regiment ist zur Zeit nur Hptm. Schmücker vorne eingesetzt, während die anderen Bataillone in absehbarer Zeit aufgefrischt werden sollen. Die Verwundung von Hptm. Schrader war nur ganz geringfügig, dagegen hatte er einen Kraftfahrzeugunfall, bei dem er eine leichte Armverletzung davontrug. Es ist bereits wieder seit Wochen voll einsatzfähig und inzwischen zum Rgt. I versetzt worden. Es ist mir daher leider nicht möglich, Ihnen seine Anschrift mitzuteilen.

Welche Pläne Herr General hinsichtlich Ihrer weiteren Verwendung hat, kann ich Ihnen noch nicht sagen. Ich nehme aber an, dass Sie eine Aufgabe erhalten werden, die Sie völlig befriedigen wird.

Ich hoffe, dass Ihre Gesundung weiterhin Fortschritte macht und Sie bald wieder in unsere Reihen zurückkehren werden.

Mit kameradschaftlichen Grüssen und Heil Hitler verbleibe ich stets

Ihr
Böhmler

Letter of congratulations sent to Veth by Oberstleutnant Rudolf Böhmler who was the commander of Rgt.4. (Author)

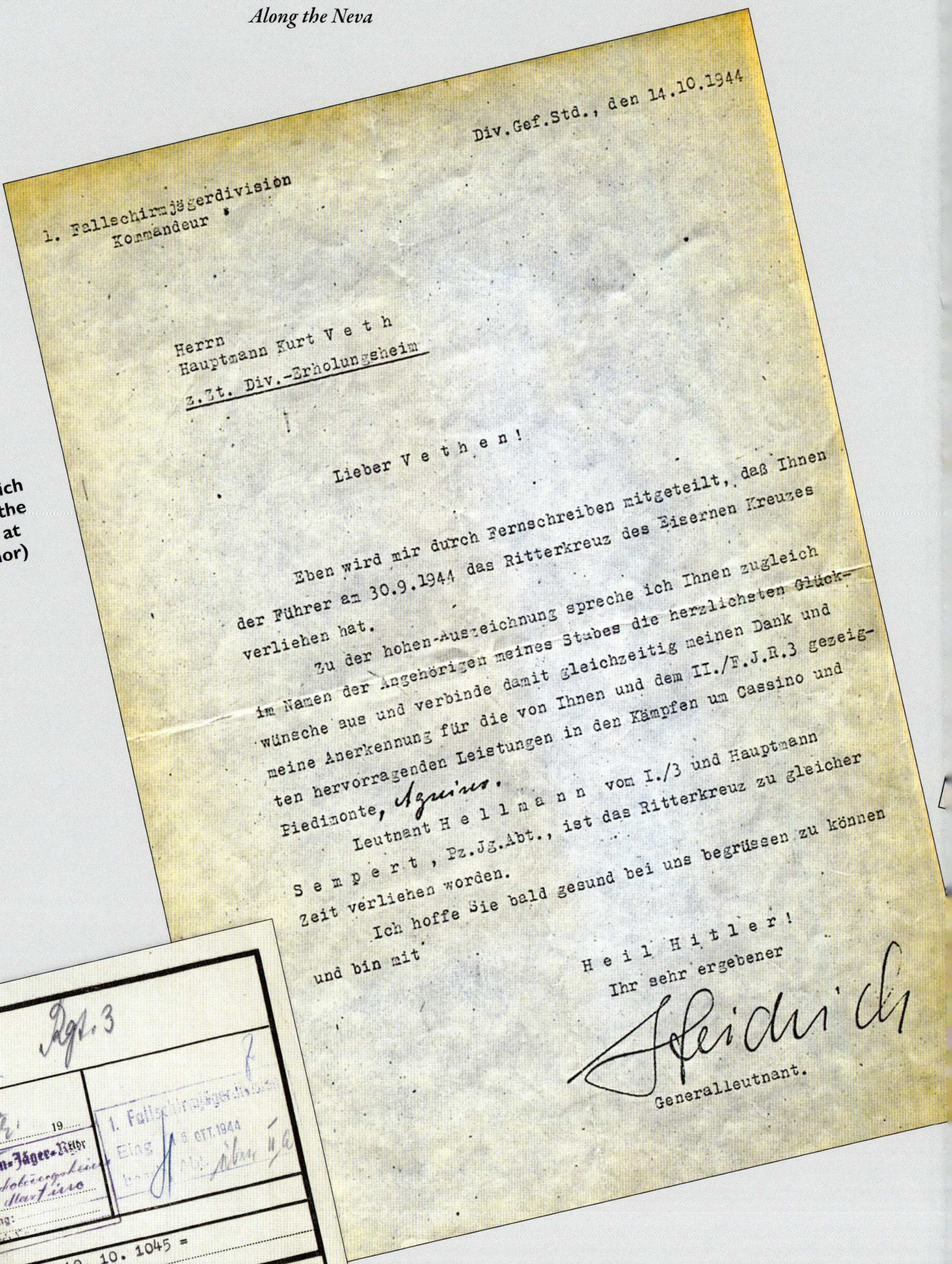

Div.Gef.Std., den 14.10.1944

1. Fallschirmjägerdivision
Kommandeur

Herrn
Hauptmann Kurt V e t h
z.Zt. Div.-Erholungsheim

Lieber V e t h e n !

Eben wird mir durch Fernschreiben mitgeteilt, daß Ihnen der Führer am 30.9.1944 das Ritterkreuz des Eisernen Kreuzes verliehen hat.

Zu der hohen Auszeichnung spreche ich Ihnen zugleich im Namen der Angehörigen meines Stabes die herzlichsten Glückwünsche aus und verbinde damit gleichzeitig meinen Dank und meine Anerkennung für die von Ihnen und dem II./F.J.R.3 gezeigten hervorragenden Leistungen in den Kämpfen um Cassino und Piedimonte, Aquino.

Leutnant H e l l m a n n vom I./3 und Hauptmann S e m p e r t , Pz.Jg.Abt., ist das Ritterkreuz zu gleicher Zeit verliehen worden.

Ich hoffe Sie bald gesund bei uns begrüssen zu können und bin mit

H e i l H i t l e r !
Ihr sehr ergebener
Heidrich
Generalleutnant.

Letter penned by General Heidrich congratulating Veth for earning the Knight's Cross in battles fought at Cassino and Piedimonte. (Author)

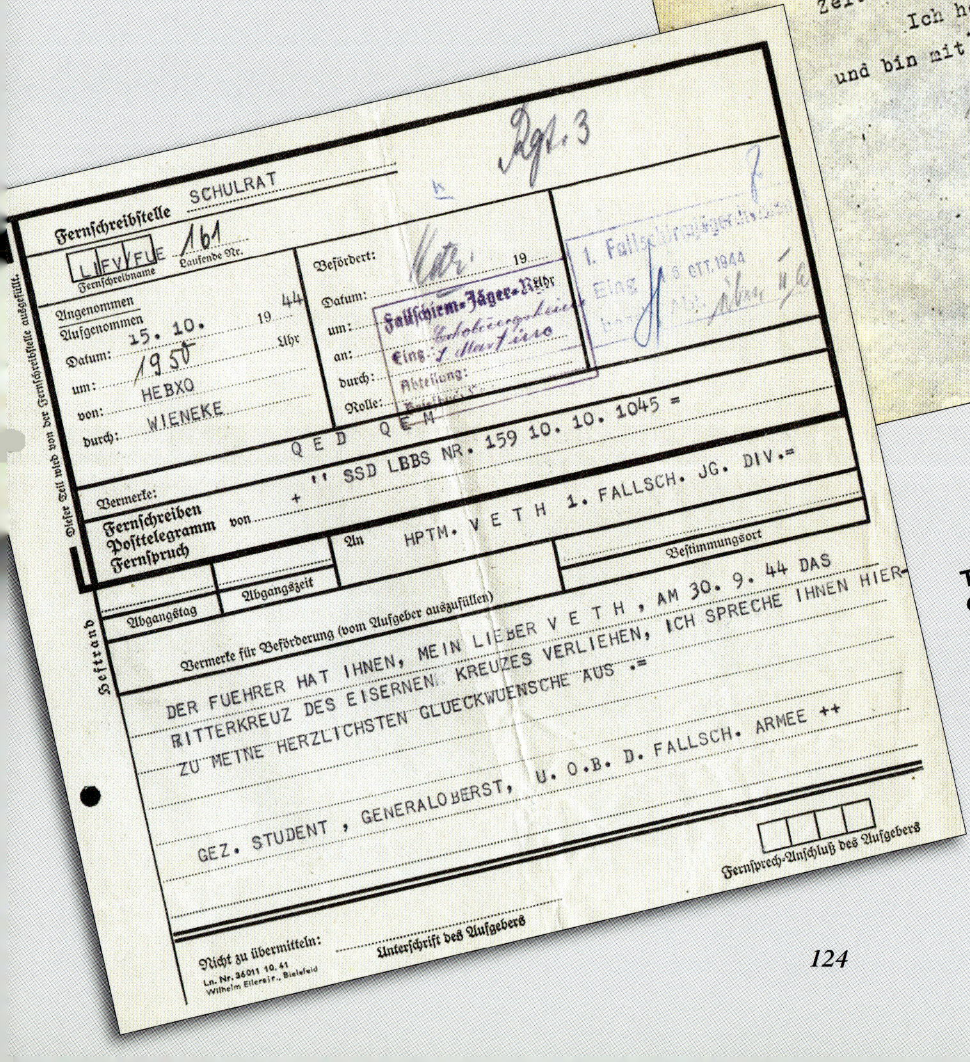

Rgt. 3

SCHULRAT

Fernschreibstelle 161
LFV/FUE
Angenommen / Aufgenommen 15. 10. 1944
Datum: 1950 Uhr
um: HEBXO
von: WIENEKE
durch:

Befördert:
Datum:
um:
an:
durch:
Rolle:

Fallschirm-Jäger-Rgt. 3
Eing.:
Abteilung:

1. Fallschirmjäger-Division
Eing. 15. OKT. 1944

QED QEH
+ '' SSD LBBS NR. 159 10. 10. 1045 =

Vermerke:
Fernschreiben / Posttelegramm / Fernspruch von
An HPTM. V E T H 1. FALLSCH. JG. DIV.=
Bestimmungsort
Abgangstag Abgangszeit

Vermerke für Beförderung (vom Aufgeber auszufüllen)

DER FUEHRER HAT IHNEN, MEIN LIEBER V E T H , AM 30. 9. 44 DAS RITTERKREUZ DES EISERNEN KREUZES VERLIEHEN, ICH SPRECHE IHNEN HIERZU MEINE HERZLICHSTEN GLUECKWUENSCHE AUS .=

GEZ. STUDENT , GENERALOBERST, U. O.B. D. FALLSCH. ARMEE ++

Fernsprech-Anschluß des Aufgebers

Nicht zu übermitteln: Unterschrift des Aufgebers

Telex sent by Generaloberst Kurt Student on October 15, 1944: "The Führer has awarded you, my dear Veth, the Knight's Cross of the Iron Cross on 30.09.44. I therefore send you my heartfelt congratulations." (Author)

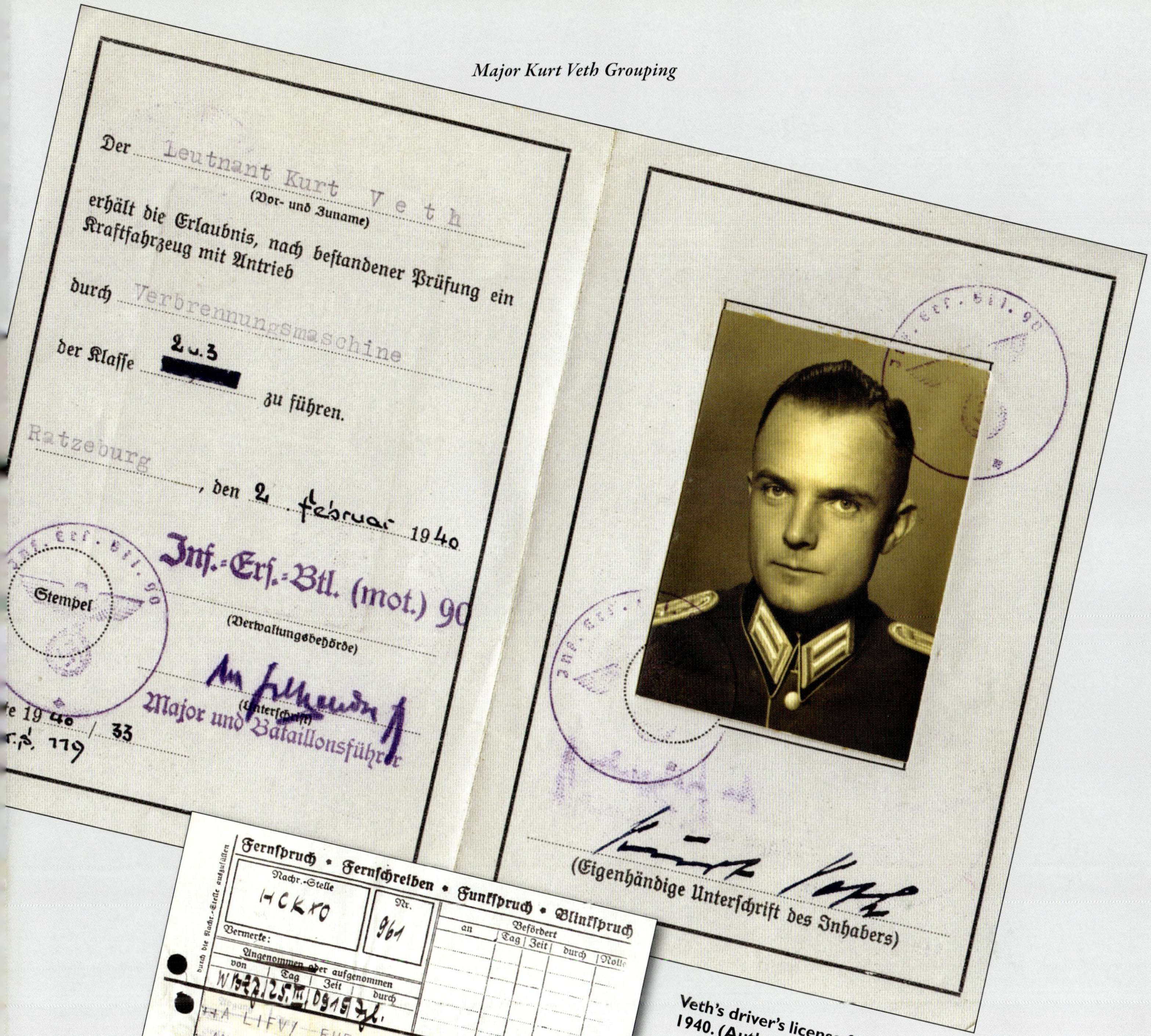

Der Leutnant Kurt Veth
(Vor- und Zuname)
erhält die Erlaubnis, nach bestandener Prüfung ein Kraftfahrzeug mit Antrieb
durch Verbrennungsmaschine
der Klasse 2 u. 3
zu führen.
Ratzeburg, den 2. Februar 1940
Stempel
Inf.-Ers.-Btl. (mot.) 90
(Verwaltungsbehörde)
(Unterschrift)
Major und Bataillonsführer
(Eigenhändige Unterschrift des Inhabers)

Veth's driver's license from February 1940. (Author)

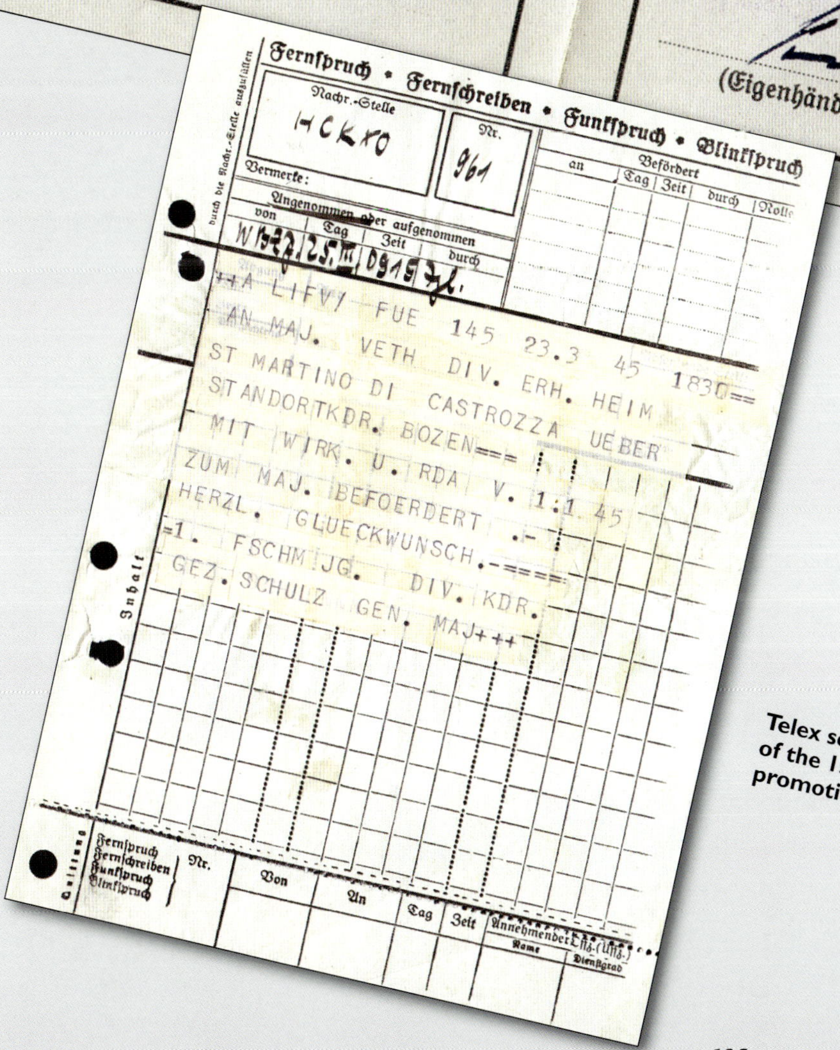

Fernspruch • Fernschreiben • Funkspruch • Blinkspruch
Nachr.-Stelle HCKXO
Nr. 961
Vermerke:
++A LIFV/ FUE 145 23.3 45 1830==
AN MAJ. VETH DIV. ERH. HEIM
ST MARTINO DI CASTROZZA UEBER
STANDORTKDR. BOZEN===
MIT WIRK. U. RDA V. 1.1.45
ZUM MAJ. BEFOERDERT .-
HERZL. GLUECKWUNSCH.-===
=1. FSCHM.JG. DIV.KDR.
GEZ. SCHULZ GEN. MAJ+++

Telex sent by Karl Lothar Schulz, commander of the 1st Paratroop Division, with news of the promotion to Major. (Author)

Abbreviations

Abt.	Abteilung	Detachment
Art.	Artillerie	Artillery
Brig.	Brigade	Brigade
Btl.	Bataillon	Battalion
Div.	Division	Division
Kpf.Grp.	Kampfgruppe	Task Force
Kdr.	Kommandeur	Commander
Kp.	Kompanie	Company
LKW	Lastkraftwagen	Truck
Pak	Panzerabwehrkanone	Anti-Tank gun
Pi.	Pioniere	Engineer
Rgt.	Regiment	Regiment
San.	Sanitäter	Corpsman
Zg.Fhr.	Zugführer	Platoon Leader

Author's Note

I am searching for original photos and documents relating to the Fallschirmjäger in North Africa and the paratroopers of I./Rgt.3 at the Neva front. Please feel free to contact me at edgar.alcidi@gmail.com. Thank you.